The Colorful World of
BALLET

CLEMENT CRISP
and
EDWARD THORPE

OCTOPUS

CONTENTS

This edition first published in 1978 by
Octopus Books Limited
59 Grosvenor Street
London W.1

© 1977 Hennerwood Publications Limited

ISBN 0 904230 39 2

Produced by Mandarin Publishers Limited
Hong Kong

INTRODUCTION

'It is the movement of people and things which consoles us. If the leaves on the trees didn't move, how sad the trees would be – and so should we.' The French painter Degas, who loved to draw dancers, wrote this in a letter, and it contains a truth about the art of ballet that explains something of the enormous popularity of dance today. From having been an entertainment of kings and courts and the audiences in a few great opera houses, ballet became great popular entertainment, and today is watched and enjoyed throughout the world. It is the only theatre art that knows no barriers of language, and it can express a multitude of ideas, moods and themes, as well as stressing the sheer beauty of movement.

We cannot hope to cover all the wide variety of dance within the confines of one book. What we hope to have done is to convey something of the excitement and satisfaction to be gained from watching dancing, and also to give some introduction to the history that lies behind the movements of the dancers. In ballet we are watching the human body at its most beautiful; the training and making of dancers is concerned with the development of a body to as near perfect as it is possible to become. Correct physique, intelligence and, above all, talent, are the raw materials which arduous daily training, continued throughout the dancer's whole career, seeks to perfect. Dancing is rooted, ultimately, in everyday movement: what the theatre has done – what ballet has done – is to extend and develop those basic human movements of walking, running, leaping and turning, and refine them into the language of an art-form. So, when we watch dancers, we watch almost super-human people, whose actions we can understand and enjoy even if we cannot copy them, just as we do the skill of cricketers, or tennis-players, or footballers, or any sportsmen. It is a good idea to start looking at ballet as a marvellous display of athletic skills. Some people are put off because they think they have got to 'understand' or look for some hidden meaning. That is the wrong approach: look at ballet as you would look at the Olympic Games, and you will immediately enjoy it, and with enjoyment comes understanding of the beauties of dancing.

CLEMENT CRISP
EDWARD THORPE

To Kenneth MacMillan and the artists of the Royal Ballet – in gratitude

Illustrated left Rudolf Nureyev and Natalya Makarova in the *Black Swan pas de deux* in Act 3 of *Swan Lake*.

Previous page Ballet Rambert in *Embrace Tiger and return to Mountain*.

Page 1 Rudolf Nureyev in *Raymonda* with American Ballet Theatre.

Acknowledgements
This book would not have been possible without the help and cooperation of many people, in particular Miss Carol Venn, Miss Maryon Lane, Miss Briony Brind, Mr Paul Tomkinson and Mr Anthony Crickmay. We are also grateful to Mr Peter Brownlee, Miss Susan Merret, Mr Tony Barlow and to all the photographers who have helped find material for this book.

THE FOUNDATIONS OF BALLET

Mankind has always danced. He expresses himself through movement and when he shows his emotions it is often gestures rather than words that tell what he feels. There are cave paintings from prehistory that suggest how those very first artists were trying to capture the excitement of movement as they hunted for food, and in primitive communities today tribes dance to invoke rain, to placate their gods or to celebrate some festival. In Ancient Egypt and in classical Greece the dance was in very early times a way of worshipping the gods, and from these rituals there developed the basic elements of all our present theatre. These are the grass-roots of dancing as it is today, but it was during the Renaissance that the foundations of what we call ballet were laid.

The Renaissance, as its name implies, was a time of rebirth, of philosophy and science and the arts. This was in no small part due to the fact that Italy was still, in the 14th and 15th centuries, made up of small states whose rulers were eager to show off their power and prestige. These dukes and princes vied with each other as patrons of the arts, and they tried to make their courts as brilliant and artistically rich as possible. This meant displays which would impress both the populace and their fellow rulers, and great families like the Medicis in Florence, and the Sforzas in Milan indulged in elaborate and opulent festivities on every suitable occasion. Some took the form of parades of decorated floats, some of masquerades and religious processions, and what became known as 'dinner ballets'. It was essential for the members of these Italian ducal courts to dance well, and at the beginning of the 15th century dancing masters were travelling the length of the country producing and teaching dances for great occasions – weddings, political alliances, and victories in war. They also wrote text-books on dancing, and the earliest treatise we have of this kind is by Domenico of Piacenza (who was in the service of the d'Este family in Ferrara), written very early in the 15th century. These text-books showed not only how to perform steps but also included arrangements of steps in carefully organized dances.

So it is in such court entertainments, with their aristocratic participants, that we can see the origins of ballet. A good example is the 'dinner ballet' staged at Tortona in 1489 to celebrate the marriage of Galeazzo, Duke of Milan, to Isabella of Aragon. It was arranged by Bergonzio di Botta, a dancing master, and we might consider it as not unlike a very extravagant and elaborate dinner dance and cabaret of today. As each course of the wedding banquet was brought in, dancers appeared impersonating the mythological characters associated with the dish. Roast lamb was attended by men who represented

---

La Camargo – portrait by Lancret. Marie Anne de Cupis de Camargo was born in Brussels in 1710. Her father was a musician and dancing master, and by the age of 16 the enchantingly pretty Marie Anne had made her début at the Paris Opéra. Her brilliance and the vivacity of her dancing excited a great deal of public admiration, and this was increased when, during a later performance, she noticed that a male dancer was not on stage at the moment he was due to execute a solo variation. She promptly improvised a dance, and the audience greeted her skill with tremendous enthusiasm. The fact that she replaced a male dancer is some indication of her quality of lightness and speed: it was her ambition to be able to move more freely than was customary for female dancers, and to rival men in ease of dancing. To do this, and to show off her feet in beaten steps, she had

the audacious idea of shortening her skirts to a few inches above the ankle. When the furore had subsided, the fashion became the norm for dancers, but it is Camargo who had struck the first blow for the ballerina's virtuosity. Her great rival Marie Sallé (1707–1756) posessed totally different gifts; she was dramatic and impassioned with a noble presence. It is noticeable, across the years, that two ballerinas often complement rather than rival each other: Taglioni and Elssler are examples from the romantic age.

La Camargo was much loved and much fêted throughout her career: she gave her last performance in 1751, and spent her retirement surrounded by dogs, cats and parrots until her death in 1770. She is remembered today in the kitchens as well as in the ballet world: the great chef Escoffier invented an iced pudding called a *bombe Camargo*.

Left Costume for a horse ballet (attributed to
Jean Berain (1637–1711), one of the chief
stage artists to the court during the reign of
Louis XIV. The art of horsemanship, like that
of ballet, had its origins in Italy, and it is not
surprising that these two arts were combined
in open-air displays: the *trionfi* of the
Renaissance. *Trionfi* were spectacular
entertainments, inspired by the 'Triumphs' of
Ancient Rome which were accorded to
generals and Emperors after a great military
success.

In the Middle Ages, the tourney or jousting
match was popular; later magnificent mock
combats were staged in an open space, or a
public square, with both horses and riders
dressed with fantastic complication. The
horses were also trained to walk and prance
through set patterns, very carefully planned
and 'choreographed'. In Italy famous horse-
ballets were staged in Florence in the early
17th century; equally famous ones were seen
in Stockholm and Vienna – where the elegant
manoeuvres of the Spanish Riding School and
its Lippizaner horses are a direct descent from
this tradition of horse-ballet. In France the
most celebrated horse-ballet was the
Carrousel of 1662, staged to celebrate the
birth of King Louis XIV's first son. (In
America today, a 'carousel' is a roundabout
with horses.) In the *Carrousel* of 1662 the
King and his brother, and three of the greatest
aristocrats of the court, each led a squadron
of horsemen who competed in tilting with
lances. Each squadron was gorgeously
dressed, both horses and riders. 'They were,
like all the rest, dazzling in their costumes
with gold and silver and precious stones
glittering against satin clothes. The trappings
of the horses were no less luxurious' (thus it
was described by a contemporary writer).
The *Carrousel* took place in the great square
in front of the Palace of the Tuileries in Paris,
which is now destroyed, although the square
acquired the name of *Place du Carrousel* in
honour of the event, and retains it to this day.

Jason and the Argonauts on their quest for the Golden Fleece; Neptune and sea sprites
entered to announce the arrival of the fish course; Pomona, goddess of plenty, presided
over the presentation of fruit. And at the end of the banquet a further allegorical 'ballet'
celebrated the joys of matrimony, combining speech, song and dance.

Such displays were soon being copied in other European courts, and particularly in
France the 'dinner ballet' was developed even further. Court entertainments became
increasingly elaborate and the 'court ballets' (*ballets de cour*) emerged which were most
splendid occasions, often presented with the express intention of conveying some
political message to the court, to distinguished guests and to other rulers about the power
of the monarch or the advisability of an alliance. Under Queen Catherine de Medicis
these entertainments became very important. As dowager Queen of France and a power
behind the throne of her three sons who each in turn became King of France (François II,
Charles IX, and Henri III), she employed court ballets to distract members of the Royal
household, and to impress foreign envoys. The 'Polish Ballet' of 1573 was devised to
celebrate the election of the Queen's third son to the throne of Poland, with declama-
tions and dancing by the ladies of the court. And in 1581, the most famous of these
festivities, *Le Ballet Comique de la Reine*, took place in Paris. It celebrated a royal marriage,
and it lasted from ten at night until three o'clock the next morning.

It was an extravagantly costly production, devised by an Italian violinist and dancing
master – Balthazar de Beaujoyeux – who had come to the court of Queen Catherine from

Left Design for a male dancer in a French *ballet de cour*, about 1660 by Henry Gissey (1621–1673). This figure represents a warrior: the sword he wears and the tunic with its decorative surcoat, the plumed head-dress and general elaboration of dress convey something of the opulence of the *ballets de cour* at the time of Louis XIV. It seems likely that the character is a noble warrior in one of the many *entrées* in the ballets in which members of the court impersonated figures from classical mythology or legend.

Right above *The Marriage of Peleus and Thetis*, Paris 1654. This four-hour spectacle was one of the first opera-ballets, and it was performed before the young King Louis XIV. Its splendid designs, by the Italian artist Giacomo Torelli, were part of the new grandeur in production: the opera-ballet was performed in one of the largest halls of the Louvre. The illustration shows the battle scene in which a danced combat was staged.

Below Illustration from Cesare Negri's text book of dancing, *Nuovi Invenzioni di Ballo*, which appeared in 1604. We see here a court gentleman practising a step which is an ancestor of the movements dancers learn in class today: to help him as a support he has what looks like a bell-pull on the left of the picture. Cesare Negri was born in Milan in 1530, and he achieved the unusual distinction of dancing on board a battle-ship to entertain the victorious admirals after the sea-battle of Lepanto in 1571.

Below right This engraving (1681) shows the stage picture during a performance of Lully's opera-ballet *Le Triomphe de l'Amour*. It is famous in the annals of ballet as the first work in which professional female dancers (as opposed to high-born amateurs) appeared. Mlle de Lafontaine and her three companions – Mlles Fanon, Roland and Lepeintre – took to the stage, and the history of the ballerina began. We know little about Mlle de Lafontaine except that she danced for ten years, and then became a nun.

Milan 30 years before and who had staged many of the court festivities for her. With its combination of song, speech, dance and quite complex productions (using 'machines', which allowed the performers to descend as from the clouds, or appear in magical transformations) the 'Ballet comique' – called *comique* not because it was funny, but because it was dramatic – was a grand example of a court spectacular. It must be remembered, though, that the performers were all members of the nobility, and their dances were so arranged as to show off elaborate patterns rather than any complication of steps. The inter-weaving of the courtiers in carefully planned loops and circles must have looked rather like the 'Formation Dancing' sometimes seen on television today. The dances were staged in the great halls of the palace, and the watching members of the court would stand or be seated on raised galleries at the sides of the hall, while the actual dances were always so performed that they faced the royal presence – the king and his guests who were seated on a dais at one end of the hall.

The monarch was also eventually to take part in certain court ballets, as well as joining in the ordinary social dancing – Queen Elizabeth I of England was famous for enjoying the high-stepping dance called *La Volta* in which she was lifted into the air. The king especially associated with court ballet is Louis XIV of France (1638–1715). He became king at the age of five, and when he was twelve he had made his first appearance taking a role in a court ballet. He was an enthusiastic dancer, and during the early years of his reign the court ballet reached its zenith. Significantly, Louis earned his title of 'The Sun King' from his role as the Sun in *Le Ballet Royal de la Nuit* in 1653 – an entertainment which was given with the express intention of glorifying the king's power and warning any possible enemies of his unassailable might.

Louis XIV employed some of the most distinguished writers, musicians, and artists of his time to devise and decorate these magnificent spectacles for him. He founded the *Académie Royale de Danse* in 1661, and eight years later he instituted the *Académie Royale de Musique*, which we know today as the Paris Opéra. On his retirement from dancing in 1670 a vital change came over the world of dance. With the king now no longer

appearing, his courtiers felt less inclined to perform, and the way was open for professional dancers to take over the presentation of ballets and to transfer them from the court to the theatres.

Among the king's entourage of artists who helped in the production of court ballets were the Italian Jean Baptiste Lully, and Pierre Beauchamps. Lully had begun his career as a dancer, but his gift for music soon earned him the position of leader of the king's violins; Beauchamps had been the king's dancing master. By 1672 these two found themselves responsible for the staging of the opera-ballets which now became the standard fare at the *Académie Royale de Musique* in Paris. The opera-ballet was to remain the most usual form of entertainment at that theatre for more than half a century.

Professional dancers were being trained – in 1713 a dance school was established at the *Académie Royale de Musique* – and already by this time the first professional female dancers had appeared. In 1681 four 'ballerinas' took the stage in Lully's opera-ballet *The Triumph of Love* and by the beginning of the 18th century the female dancer was growing in importance. Male dancers retained their supremacy because of the freedom of movement afforded by their clothes – it was easier for men to execute the increasingly complex steps found in ballet with their legs unencumbered in breeches and hose than for the women in their long voluminous skirts. But in the 1730s one female dancer decided to show off her technique. The five positions of the feet – still the basis of ballet today – had been accepted as the first essential for dancing by the beginning of the century, and already beaten steps like the *entrechat* (a rapid crossing of the feet during a jump) were being performed by men. Marie Camargo had mastered this trick, and in order to show off her twinkling feet she shortened her skirt to a discreet length above the ankle. Her contemporary, Marie Sallé, also made her mark in ballet; not by virtuosity, but by her acting and her expressive power. But throughout this century, it is the man who is the more important figure. Probably the most celebrated male dancer of the first half of the century was Gaëtano Vestris (1729–1808), Italian born, insufferably vain, and such a virtuoso that he was nicknamed 'the God of the Dance'. His son, Auguste (1760–1842) succeeded him as a star dancer and popular hero, both in France and throughout Europe (the dancing families of this time, like other troupes of entertainers and musicians, were itinerant, performing in theatres in many countries).

Garden scene from *Psammi, Re d'Egitto*: a tragic ballet by Salvatore Viganò staged at the Teatro alla Scala, Milan, in 1817. A magnificent setting, in the Egyptian style, by Alessandro Sanquirico makes great use of perspective for this view of the gardens at Memphis. *Psammis, King of Egypt* was one of Viganò's elaborate, mimed ballets, and the success of many such spectacles was, according to the great French writer, Stendhal, due in part to the superlative designs which were changed for each act, or even each scene. Stendhal also observed that the theatre itself was financed by the adjoining gambling rooms, until this practice was stopped by the ruling Austrian authorities (Italy was at this time under the domination of the Austrian Empire). Of *Psammi*, like all Viganò's ballets, nothing remains today but such illustrations, which suggest how visually exciting they must have been.

This beautiful design is by Alessandro Sanquirico (1780–1849), and it shows the conservatory which featured, somehow or other, in the action of a 'mimed character ballet' called *Elerz and Zulmida*. The work was choreographed by Louis Henry (1784–1836) who worked both in his native France and in Italy. *Elerz and Zulmida* was staged in Milan, at the Teatro alla Scala in 1826 and the score was by Pugni, who was later to work in London (he composed the music for the *Pas de Quatre*) and in Russia. The actual story of the ballet is completely unknown to us. It was plainly a 'contemporary' drama – the women's clothes are day dress of the period; the men are in military costume – probably Austrian. Sanquirico was the greatest stage decorator of his time and the magnificent scale of his designs was completely in accord with the grandiloquent mime-dramas which were staged at La Scala by Viganò.

As important as the dancers by the middle of the 18th century was the growing band of choreographers – the actual creators of the dances. These choreographers who were to be responsible for the separation of ballet from the song and recitative which had up to now been actually combined in the opera-ballet. Their aim was to make dance capable of dramatic narrative. With the development of dance technique brought about by professional performers, came the need for ballet to find itself a more truthful and expressive form. In short, the aim was to give meaning to dance movement. The usual term for this danced narrative is *ballet d'action*. The man who most clearly defined *ballet d'action* in his writings (*Letters on Dancing: 1760*) as well as in his ballets, was Jean Georges Noverre (1727–1810). Noverre, in common with several other choreographers of his time, staged his ballets throughout Europe in Stuttgart, Vienna, and France. (It was thanks to his one-time pupil, the Austrian Archduchess Marie Antoinette, who later became Queen of France, that Noverre finally was appointed as chief ballet-master at the Paris Opéra.) His influence was considerable, and it was one of his pupils, Jean Dauberval, who, in 1789, staged *La Fille mal Gardée* in Bordeaux. The originality of this ballet lay in its presentation of 'real' people – simple farming folk – as opposed to the conventional classic heroes and heroines who were featured in most of the *ballets d'action*. Unfortunately nothing remains of the choreography.

Another one of Dauberval's pupils was Salvatore Viganò (1769–1821) an Italian choreographer whose greatest works were staged at La Scala, Milan. He aimed at massive spectacles which put into practice Noverre's ideals of dramatic expression, but these were often static mime displays rather than true danced dramas.

The French Revolution, followed by 20 years of European war and then increasing industrialization had an inevitable effect upon the performing arts.

By the turn of the century artists of all kinds were beginning to react against the ideas and rigid forms of the 18th century. In literature, music and painting new themes emerged, and emotion became more appealing than reason in art. The writings of Byron and Sir Walter Scott and of the German poet Heine; the music and writings of Hoffmann; the paintings of Delacroix, the music of Schubert, Chopin, Berlioz, are all prime examples of this vital change of direction. And of course ballet, which was a synthesis of music, painting, dance and theatre, was affected too.

ROMANTICISM AND THE CLASSICS

In June 1827 a young dancer arrived in Paris. She was accompanied by her brother, who was also a dancer, and her father, a ballet-master. She was Marie Taglioni, a member of one of the several itinerant dancing families of the period – families who moved from country to country, staging ballets and performing in them. Marie had been born in Stockholm in 1804 – her mother was Swedish, her father Italian – and during a childhood spent wandering round Europe, her father, Filippo Taglioni, had given her a rigorous ballet training which was ultimately to produce a dancer of unique and completely new qualities. She was a thin, plain child, with long arms and legs, and though she did not in the least resemble the conventionally pretty dancers of her time, her father had so developed her abilities, stressing lightness, grace and charm, that she had become a very gifted and original performer. Unlike her contemporaries, Marie Taglioni looked demure, delicate and discreetly charming when she danced. There was no obvious 'showing-off' in her movements, yet her technique was to become more complete than that of any previous ballerina.

In due course Filippo Taglioni brought his family to Paris – then the centre of the dance world – and in 1827 Marie made her Opéra début, dancing a pas de deux with her brother: and the future of ballet was changed. Grace such as hers had never been seen on stage before: here was an ideal of poetic sensibility in motion, ethereal, weightless, decorous. A new 'Romantic' style had arrived in ballet, and almost at once the other ballerinas of the time were made to look dated and slightly vulgar. It is no accident that a new verb soon entered the vocabulary of the dance-world: *taglioniser* – which meant 'to dance like Taglioni'. Marie's fame spread throughout Europe, but it was not until 1832, with *La Sylphide*, that she was recognized as the absolute queen of the Romantic ballet.

In the previous year, in Meyerbeer's opera *Robert the Devil*, which was staged at the Opéra, Taglioni had appeared in a dance scene set in a moonlit cloister, taking the role of the ghost of an abbess who leads a group of white-clad nuns in a spectral dance. Here was one of the great images of Romanticism – an artistic movement which was pre-occupied with the supernatural, with shadows, mists and moonlight, with ghosts, witches, hobgoblins and fairies. The moonlight effects were now possible in the theatre thanks to the introduction of gaslight, and the mysterious effects which could be achieved were an essential part of the ballets of the next two decades. It was the tenor who sang the lead in *Robert the Devil* who first had the idea of a ballet to show off Marie Taglioni in this new style, and in 1832 Marie's father created *La Sylphide* (see page 16).

This Opéra staging of *La Sylphide* was an immense triumph, and the image of Taglioni in this role was one which was to haunt ballerinas for the rest of the century. Taglioni's ethereal grace, her soaring flights and graceful deportment set the seal on the establishment of a new epoch for ballet. Her costume, too, was all but revolutionary: a tight bodice and billowing white tarlatan skirts were an important development in dress for female dancers. It was an age obsessed with the female dancer, and led to the almost total eclipse of the male, who was eventually relegated to the ignoble task of simply carrying the ballerina about the stage. For 20 years, until her retirement in 1847, Marie Taglioni was the supreme embodiment of the Romantic ballerina, and started the public passion for ballerina worship; in Russia a group of balletomanes acquired a pair of her shoes, had them cooked and served with a sauce, and ate them.

These shoes were not the blocked shoes of today, but simple satin slippers with a light sole. To encompass the new development of 'point-work' – dancing on the tips of the toes – which gave such an illusion of lightness as the ballerina seemingly skimmed the stage, the dancers' toes were protected by cotton wadding. Point-work was the best-known innovation of Romantic ballet, but its use did not become general until later in the

Natalya Bessmertnova of the Bolshoy ballet is seen in a happy moment from the first act of *Giselle,* when the peasant girl dances with her friends.

century when stronger, stiffened shoes were developed by the Italians to enable ballerinas to perform toe-work of increasing brilliance.

Taglioni's version of *La Sylphide* has been lost: the staging we know today is due to the Danish dancer and ballet-master August Bournonville (1805–1879). Bournonville studied in Paris with Auguste Vestris, and saw Taglioni dancing there – he found in her his ideal dancer. When he returned to Copenhagen in 1830 to take over the direction of the Royal Danish Ballet, Bournonville was faced with a major task of reviving a feeble ballet company. This he did by inspired teaching, preserving all he had learned from Vestris, and by creating nearly 40 ballets for his Danish company until his retirement in 1877. (This Bournonville inheritance is still the basis of the Danish Royal Ballet's present repertory training, with its light buoyant style of dancing.) In 1836 Bournonville decided to make his own version of *La Sylphide* for his favourite young pupil, the 17-year-old Lucile Grahn. He had a new score written, but more important was the fact that he

Left Fanny Elssler in *La Tarentule*. Lithograph by J. Bouvier 1840. This comic ballet was first staged by the French choreographer Jean Coralli at the Paris Opéra in 1839, as a vehicle for Fanny Elssler. She was cast as Lauretta, an Italian village girl who is forced into a betrothal with a quack doctor, since only by this sacrifice will he cure Luigi, Lauretta's fiancé, of a tarantula bite. To delay the

marriage, she plays all kinds of tricks on the old doctor – even feigning to have been bitten by a tarantula herself. Eventually Luigi resolves matters by discovering the doctor's wife and Lauretta and Luigi are united as the doctor is chased from the village.

The most celebrated number in the ballet was her Tarantella in Act 1. The Tarantella is a southern Italian dance of great liveliness: supposedly the dance is a cure for the dreadful frenzy which follows the bite of a tarantula – by energetic exercise the spider's venom is overcome.

Above Marie Taglioni in *La Gitana*. Lithograph by J. Bouvier published in 1839. In 1839 Antonio Guerra, an Italian choreographer, came to London to restage a ballet that Filippo Taglioni had made the year before for his daughter in St Petersburg. This was *La Gitana* (The Gypsy Girl). In it Marie Taglioni undertook a part which was the exact opposite of her drifting sylphide. She played the role of a girl stolen as a child from her aristocratic parents and brought up by gypsies. The purpose of the work was to show her off in dances of a lively character, and although much of the music was based upon the mazurka, which would have been familiar to

Russian audiences, the highlight of the ballet was a Spanish dance, in the fashion of the *cachucha*. Taglioni as the heroine, hearing this Spanish music which was familiar from her childhood, moved audiences by what N. P. Willis, a critic of the time, said was 'the finest piece of pantomimic acting I ever saw'. In this dance, of course, she was challenging Fanny Elssler (famous also for her cachucha in *The Devil on Two Sticks*) on the same ground, but Taglioni's artistry was thought greater than that of all her rivals. N. P. Willis goes on: 'Taglioni alone "finishes" the step or the pirouette, or the arrowy bound over the scene, as calmly, as accurately, as faultlessly as she begins it. She floats out of a pirouette as if, instead of being made giddy, she had been lulled by it into a smiling and child-like dream, and instead of trying herself and her aplomb (as is seen in all other dancers, by their effort to recover composure), it had been the moment when she had rallied and had been refreshed. The smile, so expressive of enjoyment in her own grace, which steals over Taglioni's lips when she does a difficult step, seems communicated in an indefinable languor to her limbs. You cannot fancy her fatigued when, with her peculiar softness of motion, she curtsies to the applause of an enchanted audience, and walks lightly away.'

Left Marie Taglioni in *La Sylphide* (Act 1) a lithograph by A. E. Chalon published in 1846. This beautiful portrait tells us a great deal about this famous dancer and also about the Romantic movement of which she was the incarnation. Taglioni is seen in the moment from Act 1 of the ballet when the Sylphide appears at the window to gaze adoringly upon James. The delicate femininity and wistful charm of her pose suggest the exquisite Taglioni's appeal to audiences. Her dress shows the major innovation in costume for the ballerina that was started with *La Sylphide*: the gently billowing bell-shaped skirts of white muslin epitomised the floating, drifting qualities that were to be so necessary a part of the new image of the dancer, an image which Taglioni herself first gave to ballet. The line of the skirt gave freedom of movement, but it also reflected the coming outline of women's dress at this time (although skirts were worn to the ground off stage). The tightly waisted bodice, revealing the shoulders in a decorous manner, is a fore-runner of what was to become very fashionable in early Victorian times: the coronet of roses and the flowered corsage, the pearl necklace and pearl bracelets are also essential Victorian additions. *La Sylphide* inspired many fashions: bonnets, coats, and parasols, and even materials, were advertised in newspapers '*à La Sylphide*'. The descent from the window ledge on which the Sylphide is standing was achieved – and still is in current stagings – by a small moveable platform set against the scenery on which the Sylphide poses on point and is gently lowered to stage level. She seems to be drifting gently to the ground as if by magic, and it was Taglioni's genius as a dancer which suggested that when she performed she did, indeed, drift from the air to the earth. She was sometimes called 'the spirit of the air'.

preserved the importance of the male dancer, since he was himself an exceptionally gifted performer. Almost alone in Europe, Bournonville insisted upon the proper balance between male and female dancing in his ballets.

Elsewhere the adulation of the ballerina had become almost a mania. At the Paris Opéra the astute manager of the theatre, Dr Véron, engineered and encouraged a rivalry between the established star Taglioni and a newcomer, the beautiful and dramatic Fanny Elssler. Elssler was born in Vienna in 1810, and she made her Paris début in 1834. Her style was voluptuous, in direct contrast to the chaste Taglioni, and Véron encouraged the public to take sides in championing these two very different artists. Théophile Gautier, the poet and outstanding critic of ballet at this time, called Taglioni a 'Christian dancer' and Elssler 'a pagan'. Elssler's hold over the public was intensified when she appeared in a new ballet *The Devil on Two Sticks*, in which she performed a Spanish dance, the *Cachucha*. This was enormously successful and became as much associated with her name as did, for example, the *Dying Swan* with Anna Pavlova at the beginning of this century. People professed to be shocked at her 'exotic' movements, but audiences thronged to see her, and when in 1837 Taglioni left to dance in Russia, Elssler remained in Paris as the star ballerina at the Opéra. Three years later, like Taglioni, she set out to conquer new audiences, who were even more enthusiastic about her intense, dramatic gifts. For two years she toured throughout the USA – so successfully that when she danced in Washington, the American congress ended its business early one day so that its members could go and watch her. She was hailed in London and Russia, and it was in St Petersburg and Moscow that public enthusiasm for her reached its zenith. At her farewell performance in Moscow, dancing in *La Esmeralda*, a ballet in which she had first triumphed in London, she was given 300 bouquets, took 42 curtain calls, and when she left the theatre the horses were unhitched from her coach and she was drawn through the streets by a team of adoring young men surrounded by an excited crowd.

With Taglioni and Elssler away on their tours, the Paris Opéra found a new heroine in the young Carlotta Grisi (1819–1899). She had been discovered in Naples as a brilliant 16-year-old soloist by Jules Perrot, himself an outstanding dancer who was soon to be recognized as the greatest choreographer of the Romantic era. Perrot fell in love with her and undertook to develop her career as a dancer, and after touring round Europe the couple arrived in Paris in 1840. They appeared at a minor theatre in a divertissement called *Le Zingaro*, and Carlotta, who was a member of a distinguished family of opera singers, also sang in this production. She was next invited to appear at the Opéra, where she danced a new pas de deux, but it was Théophile Gautier, who had fallen in love with her, who was to be instrumental in devising the ballet which was to make her name immortal.

The Story of
LA SYLPHIDE

The story is set in Scotland, considered a remote and romantic place by the public of the time, and it concerns James, a young crofter on the eve of his marriage to Effie, a pretty village girl. At curtain rise James is seen asleep in a fireside chair in his farmhouse; by his side kneels a forest sprite, the sylphide. She gazes adoringly at him, and when he awakes he is immediately bewitched by her mysterious child-like grace. She tells him of her love for him and he falls under her spell. He is now torn between his earthly fiancée, Effie, and the charm of his supernatural love. Throughout the preparations for the wedding James is haunted by the sprite as she flits about the stage – there are delightful theatrical effects in which she disappears from a chair, floats down from a window, and at one moment, whisks up the chimney to avoid detection by Gurn, a rival for Effie's hand. In the midst of the wedding celebrations a strange old woman appears. This is Madge, a witch. She is a fortune teller, and she takes pleasure in telling Effie that she will never marry James, but is destined to be Gurn's bride. Infuriated, James drives her from the farmhouse; but the sylphide still lures him on, and eventually he follows her away to the hills, leaving Effie distraught and alone.

The second act of the ballet begins with Madge and a coven of witches brewing something evil in a cauldron – a poisoned scarf with which Madge intends to destroy both the sylphide and James. The action then moves to a forest glade where James and the sylphide dance together. She brings him water, fruit and even a bird's nest, as tokens of her love and her sister sylphides dance around the couple. Madge now enters bearing the scarf which she hands to James. The sylphide sees the scarf and begs James to give it to her, and as he folds it round her shoulders the evil spell takes its effect. She is seized with the chill of death; her wings drop off, and she dies in the arms of the agonized James. He sees her borne away to some sylphide heaven by her companions, and Madge exults in triumph. At the same moment she shows James the wedding procession of Effie and Gurn on their way to the church. James collapses to the ground: he has lost both his earthly love and his supernatural beloved.

Left La Sylphide. In 1973 Scottish Ballet presented a careful and charming production of Bournonville's *La Sylphide* which had been mounted for them by the great Danish authority on Bournonville, Hans Brenaa, with designs by Peter Cazalet. The illustration shows Sally Collard-Gentle as the sylphide and Graham Bart as James in the scene from Act 1 when the sylphide appears to James at the window: comparing this with the lithograph of Taglioni on the previous page it can be seen how strongly Taglioni's influence has survived. Bournonville, who danced with Taglioni, called her his 'ideal' dancer, and when he staged *La Sylphide* in Copenhagen in 1836 it was to star himself as James and his 17-year-old pupil Lucile Grahn as the sylphide. The excellence of the Scottish Ballet's production lies in the atmospheric quality of the company performance and in their understanding of the period style. This is an outstandingly good version of the first Romantic ballet.

Top right La Sylphide. It is, of course, the Royal Danish Ballet that produces the most authentic presentations of the Bournonville ballets, which have been kept in continuous performance since their creation in Copenhagen. For over 140 years now, Danish dancers have passed from generation to generation the essential qualities of Bournonville interpretation and technique, which is practised in the ballet classes in Copenhagen. It is very much a living tradition: two days before he died, August Bournonville hailed the first appearance of a young dancer, Hans Beck. Beck did not die until 1951, and by then he had been able to hail, in his turn, the début of a male dancer who was both an impeccable classical dancer and an ideal exponent of the Bournonville manner – Erik Bruhn. The illustration shows the Royal Danish Ballet towards the end of Act II of *La Sylphide* when the sprite is dying, having worn the poisoned scarf. Anna Laerkeson is here surrounded by grieving sylphides.

Centre Napoli. One of the great sources of ideas for August Bournonville's ballets was his foreign travel. In 1841 he was banished from Denmark, following an extraordinary scene in the theatre. One evening, as he came on stage to dance, he was greeted with a barrage of boos organized by a faction who wanted him to invite Lucile Grahn back to dance in Copenhagen (she had been appearing abroad for some years). Ignoring the demonstrators Bournonville approached the Royal Box, and asked the king whether he should continue dancing. The King told him to go on and the performance proceeded. But next morning Bournonville was arrested for having dared to approach the King during a performance and banished from Denmark for six months. This period he spent in Italy, which provided him with material for several ballets. The most important of these was the masterpiece which he created immediately on returning to Copenhagen: *Napoli*. It tells the story of a fisherman and of his beloved who is captured by a mediterranean sea-sprite who keeps her prisoner in the blue grotto in

Capri. The hero rescues her, and the final act of *Napoli* is a celebration which culminates in a phenomenal series of tarantellas. It is one of Bournonville's happiest and most dazzling displays, and the Royal Danish Ballet perform it with unparalleled zest and joyousness.

Bottom Flower Festival in Genzano. Carla Fracci and Erik Bruhn with American Ballet Theatre. Nothing remains of Bournonville's *Flower Festival in Genzano*, one of his Italian-inspired ballets, which he created in 1858, except the enchanting pas de deux. It has attractive music and is still frequently performed as a concert item. Here it is danced by another combination of Danish and Italian talent: Carla Fracci is much loved as one of the leading ballerinas of Italy, and Erik Bruhn was a supreme Bournonville stylist.

Left Giselle is undoubtedly the most widely known romantic ballet and remains one of the supreme challenges for the ballerina. It demands a superlative technique, a sense of period style, and great and compelling dramatic power to make the celebrated mad-scene at the end of Act 1 convincing to audiences. The delicate but human qualities of Giselle in Act 1 are contrasted with the ethereal, drifting Wili that she becomes in Act 2, who must try to save her beloved Albrecht. In this century many great dancers have been associated with the role, notably Olga Spessivtseva, Anna Pavlova, Alicia Markova, Galina Ulanova and Yvette Chauviré, while today's audiences are equally moved by Natalya Makarova. Here Karen Kain and Frank Augustyn are seen in Peter Wright's staging of *Giselle* for the Canadian National Ballet with designs by Desmond Heeley. Giselle's love of dancing is well captured by Miss Kain, as well as her unquestioning delight in Albrecht's love for her. Karen Kain and Frank Augustyn are the National Ballet of Canada's leading young stars. Both graduates of the company School in Toronto, they won prizes at the Moscow international ballet competition, and have achieved international acclaim. They have appeared as guest artists in Moscow and with many other companies, but their true setting is the National Ballet. Miss Kain's beautiful technique and charm, and Frank Augustyn's handsome presence are qualities that are mutually complementary in performance.

Above Natalya Makarova in Act 1 of *Giselle* with American Ballet Theatre. Natalya Makarova is generally acknowledged as the greatest Giselle of our time. She first danced the role in 1961 when a member of the Kirov Ballet in Leningrad, and she has since performed it with major companies around the world. Her interpretation is magnificent both in its dramatic sensibility and in the sheer beauty of its execution. Her ability to convey every nuance of feeling of the peasant girl in Act 1 culminates in a mad scene of tremendous intensity; the acute suffering of the girl is heartrending as her hands pick frantically at the imagined flower which she seems to hold. In Act 2 she is a wraith drifting through the air, but at the same time the emotional quality of her love for Albrecht is retained, reminding us of the human warmth of the first act. It is performances of this calibre which keep the old ballets of the 19th century alive for modern audiences: in each of Makarova's appearances in this role, as in every other one, we are aware that it has been re-thought and brought freshly to life. Miss Makarova's partnership with Anthony Dowell in her interpretations with the Royal Ballet, and with Mikhail Barishnikov with American Ballet Theatre, have already become part of the legends of dance today.

Gautier had been reading a book about Germany, and a legend in it – that of the Wilis, the dancing sprites of the Rhineland – gave him the idea for *Giselle*. This was first performed at the Opéra in June 1841. The score by Adam had been quickly composed, and although the choreography was ascribed to Jean Coralli, the resident ballet-master at the Opéra, it was known that Perrot had in fact created all the dances for Giselle and her beloved Albrecht. (See page 20 for the story of *Giselle*.)

Carlotta Grisi's beauty and charm as *Giselle* won her great acclaim, and in the following year she came to London to repeat her triumph in this ballet which was staged at Her Majesty's Theatre by Perrot and the resident ballet-master there. London showed the same enthusiasm for ballet as Paris, and Perrot's continuing presence was to sustain public interest through an important series of ballets which he mounted at Her Majesty's Theatre.

The Story of
GISELLE

The ballet is divided into two contrasting acts. The setting of the first is in a Rhineland village at the time of the grape harvest. Giselle, a simple peasant girl, is in love with Loys, a mysterious young man who shows a deep affection for her, and she cannot respond to the love that Hilarion, a woodman, also offers her. Giselle, a delicate girl, loves only two things, Loys and dancing, and her mother warns her that dancing will be her downfall. She will die and become a Wili, one of the ghostly spirits of girls who have died before their wedding day and who haunt the night, dancing to death any man they meet. Hilarion does not trust Loys; he breaks into Loy's cottage, and there discovers a nobleman's sword. He does not at first understand what this means, but when a noble hunting party arrives in the village to ask for refreshment the truth becomes clear. Loys is in fact an aristocrat, Count Albrecht, and his betrothed, Bathilde is among the hunting party. She greets him with amazement at finding him in such an unlikely spot. Giselle's subsequent realization that her beloved Loys is in fact promised to another unseats her reason. She goes mad, tries to stab herself with Albrecht's sword, and dies at his feet.

Act 2 is set in the depths of a forest, where Giselle has been buried. Hilarion is grieving at her graveside, and suddenly, as midnight sounds, he is surrounded by the ghostly forms of the Wilis, led by Myrtha their Queen. There is no escape. Relentlessly he is forced to dance into a state of exhaustion and then driven to his death in a lake. Now the Wilis gather round Giselle's grave and Myrtha summons her spirit to be initiated into their ghostly rites. They melt away as they hear a sound, and Albrecht appears, bearing flowers to lay on Giselle's tomb. As he kneels in prayer, Giselle appears to him. This seems like a dream, but suddenly it becomes a nightmare as the Wilis appear, to exact their vengeance. Myrtha condemns Albrecht to dance until he dies, but Giselle's love for him has survived death and she joins in his dances, seeking to sustain him. As Albrecht falls exhausted to the ground, near to death, the first rays of dawn filter through the trees. Daylight destroys the Wilis' power and they return to their graves, and Giselle takes a last farewell of her beloved. Though he had caused her death, her love for him has remained strong and she has saved him.

Left The *Pas de Quatre*. Lithograph by
A. E. Chalon showing Marie Taglioni, Fanny
Cerrito, Carlotta Grisi and Lucile Grahn in
Jules Perrot's divertissement at Her Majesty's
Theatre, London: July 12 1845. There they
are, poised, captured for all time in one of the
most celebrated groupings in ballet – Taglioni
stands with Cerrito on the left, Grahn and
Grisi on the right. Surrounded by a haze of
tulle, they represent the idealized image of the
ballerina as a creature of gentle ethereal grace,
caught, it seems, only for a moment on the
ground before floating away. The *Pas de
Quatre* has been re-created in recent years,
with new choreography by both Keith Lester
and Anton Dolin, and many celebrated
ballerinas have given impersonations of their
famous predecessors, notably Alicia Markova
as Taglioni and Alexandra Danilova as
Cerrito.

Opposite page, top *Giselle*. Ekatarina
Maximova in the mad-scene at the end of
Act 1, with the Bolshoy Ballet. Giselle at this
moment has become deranged after her
realization that Albrecht has deceived her.
As her mind wanders she relives all her past
happiness, and in this picture we see her
mother, on the left, kneeling in distress
surrounded by the peasants of the village,
while Albrecht (Vladimir Vasiliev) looks on
aghast at the tragedy he has caused. On the
left Hilarion can be seen, adding his entreaties
to those of Giselle's mother. The mad-scene
in *Giselle* still bears traces of Fanny Elssler's
dramatic interpretation of the 1840s. It was
Elssler, rather than Carlotta Grisi (the role's
creator), who first revealed the high emotional
possibilities of this passage, and later
interpreters have often continued this
tradition, though the scene can be played in
many different ways. The Bolshoy Ballet's
staging by Leonid Lavrovsky is remarkable for
its dramatic urgency, and Ekaterina Maximova
and Vladimir Vasiliev (two of the greatest
stars of the Bolshoy Ballet today) are
renowned in the leading roles.

Opposite page, below Alicia Alonso and
Cyril Atanassof in *Giselle* Act 2 at the Paris
Opéra. This picture, taken from the wings at the
Opéra, shows the pas de deux in Act 2 when
the spirit of Giselle tries to help and sustain
Albrecht as he is forced to dance by the Wilis.
Alicia Alonso, the celebrated Cuban ballerina,
has been hailed for her range of dramatic
interpretations, not only in the classics, but
also in modern roles. For many years she was
a principal ballerina of American Ballet
Theatre, but since 1955 her own company in
Cuba has been the National Ballet of that
country. Her work in Cuba has been most
impressive, and her school in Havana has
produced many distinguished dancers. It was
she who, in 1972, staged this version of
Giselle at the Opéra. Cyril Atanassoff, a
product of the Opéra School, became an
étoile (an official rank at the Opera denoting
the highest status in the company) in 1964.
He is a dancer of fine presence and elegant
technique.

Alas, nothing remains of these works, but their impact upon London's ballet-public was
testimony to their excellence. In the early years of her reign Queen Victoria was a devotee,
so much so that in 1843 she expressed a wish to see Fanny Elssler and another ballerina
who had come to prominence, Fanny Cerrito, in a pas de deux. Cerrito (1817–1909) was
born in Naples, and she had been the especial favourite of London audiences from her
first appearance there in 1840. A brilliant and sparkling dancer, she had become the darling
of society, but the decision to pair her in a duet with Elssler was to present very real
problems for Perrot, who was entrusted with creating a dance for these two idols. Elssler
had just returned from her American triumphs, and Cerrito was secure in the affection
of the London audience. Neither star wanted to open the piece – this would have implied
that the other was more important – and Perrot's solution was to create an opening
sequence in which the two divinities danced the same steps together. This pas de deux
was a sensational success, so much so that a couple of years later Benjamin Lumley, the
manager of Her Majesty's Theatre, was seized with the wild idea of featuring four of
the great ballerinas in a *pas de quatre*: Taglioni, Cerrito, Grisi and the Danish star, Lucile
Grahn. Again Perrot's ingenuity was to be put to the test, not only in composing variations
which would show off each ballerina at her best, but also in the diplomacy of ensuring that
each of these very jealous and proud ladies did not seem to be less favourably treated
than any of the others. All seemed to go well in rehearsals: Taglioni as the senior dancer,
naturally was given pride of place and danced the last solo, and Grahn as the most junior
would start the solos. But how to decide on the precedence between Cerrito and Grisi
was a dreadful problem. Neither lady wished to appear before the other, and Perrot was
at his wit's end. Fortunately Lumley thought of the ideal solution: let the oldest take her
rightful position and go second. When this was told to Cerrito and Grisi, they smiled
sweetly and offered the senior position to each other, and it was Perrot who was allowed
to decide.

The *Pas de Quatre*, once announced, aroused intense enthusiasm in London, and on the
night of 12 July 1845, a packed and ecstatic house watched these four goddesses of the
dance perform in graceful union. It was an enormously successful theatrical venture, and

Opposite Patricia MacBride and Peter Martins with the New York City Ballet in *Coppélia* Act 1. In 1974 George Balanchine decided to add *Coppélia* to the repertory of the New York City Ballet, which presents very few of the traditional old classics. The illustration shows Patricia MacBride and Peter Martins in the 'ear of corn' test from Act 1. Swanilda doubts if Frantz loves her, having seen him flirting with other girls. Frantz protests his love, and reminds her of the legend that if an ear of corn is shaken, the rattling of the grains will tell that love is true. Alas for poor Swanilda, the ear of corn fails to produce even the slightest sound, and she is much disappointed. The choreography of the section is very beautiful and at the end Frantz rushes after Swanilda to assure her that he can actually hear the rattle of the grains of corn. Patricia MacBride is a superlative City Ballet dancer; Peter Martins, Danish trained, is one of the company's outstanding principals.

Right The Royal Danish Ballet staged a version of *Coppélia* in 1896, but the present production is that by Harald Lander. It differs from other versions not only in choreography, and in the dramatic sense of its portrayal of the characters (in this it reflects the influence of August Bournonville), but also in the care taken with the national dances. The Royal Danes are seen here in one of the folk dances from Act 1, which contains probably the best loved music of Delibes' very loveable score.

Far right Natalya Makarova as Swanilda (*Coppélia*) with American Ballet Theatre. Swanilda is a wonderful role for a ballerina comedienne. While not demanding the same dramatic intensity as *Giselle*, it is a rewarding part: the audience is able to share Swanilda's high-spirited view of life, which is expressed not only in the tricks she plays on poor old Coppélius, but also in the ebullient choreography. But for all its humour, there is at the heart of *Coppélia* a serious theme, a girl fighting for the boy she loves, and his realization of the value of her love despite the superficial attractions of the mysterious Coppélia who turns out to be nothing but a mechanical doll. Makarova enjoys herself thoroughly in this role and we see her here in a wonderfully happy jump (a *jeté*, see chapter five). The American Ballet Theatre staging is by Enrique Martinez.

Right Ghislaine Thesmar and Michaël Denard in *Coppélia* at the Paris Opéra. Although *Coppélia* was created at the Paris Opéra, it has undergone several re-stagings there, most recently by Pierre Lacotte. In a new version he in fact sought to return to the original, and forgotten, choreography of St Léon, with the notable exception that the role of Frantz is now given to a male dancer. Up to the 1950s it had been danced by a girl, *en travesti*, rather like the principal boy in an English pantomime. The costumes and décor of this new, pretty Paris version were inspired by the original designs of 1870. Ghislaine Thesmar and Michaël Denard are both leading artists of the Opéra ballet, and they are seen in the grand pas de deux from the last act.

was to be repeated during the season, but it was remarkable in its exclusion of the male dancer. The supremacy of the ballerina implied the decline of the seriousness of ballet as a theatrical art in Western Europe. (By 1870, when *Coppélia* was first produced in Paris, it is significant that the role of Frantz, the hero, was taken by the prettiest girl in the Opéra ballet company.) In the years following the *Pas de Quatre*, Perrot staged three more starry divertissements: *The Judgement of Paris* (1846), *Les Eléments* (1847), and *The Four Seasons* (1848). However, his most important work in London was in the magnificent dramatic spectacles that he was to create: such works as *Giselle* (London 1842), *Ondine* (London 1843), *La Esmeralda* (London 1844), *Eoline* (London 1845), *Catarina* and *Lalla Rookh* (London 1846). In 1847, the public's interest was caught by the new attraction of the great Swedish singer, Jenny Lind, and opera now replaced ballet in the affection of the audience. Within a couple of years Perrot had moved on to Russia, to take up a post of ballet-master to the Imperial Russian Ballet in St Petersburg.

Ballet had taken root in Russia, thanks once again to Royal patronage, during the 18th century. Companies were established in Moscow and in St Petersburg, the capital city and chief seat of the Tsar's court. The development of training and the creation of ballets had been almost exclusively due to the presence of Italian and French ballet-masters, and the whole glorious history of ballet in Russia in the 19th century was due to a succession of French choreographers, from Didelot, who came to Russia in 1801, through Perrot, who worked there from 1849 to 1859 and St Léon, chief ballet-master from 1859 to 1869, to Marius Petipa, who arrived in 1847 and who was appointed first ballet-master in 1869 and ruled absolutely thereafter until 1903. At a time when ballet was declining in Western Europe it was developing enormously in Russia. During the latter

part of the 19th century the Romantic movement gave way to what is conveniently known as the period of 'classic' ballets. Perrot's ten years in Russia were important, in that he re-staged many of his greatest works for the Petersburg company. His successor, Arthur St Léon (1821–1870) divided his time between his native Paris and Petersburg (there was a natural affinity between Paris and Petersburg, the great westward looking capital of the Russian Empire). In the year of his death St Léon created one last enchanting and enduring work, *Coppélia*. (See following page for the story of *Coppélia*.)

Despite its abundant humour, and the enduring beauties of Delibes' wonderful score, *Coppélia* was at first associated with tragic events. It was staged in May 1870 and within a couple of months France was at war with Prussia and the next two years were a tragic time for the nation, as the siege of Paris, final defeat in the war and the downfall of the monarchy, and civil strife, took their toll. The young ballerina Giuseppina Bozzacchi, who was chosen to play Swanilda was also a victim of events. She was a brilliantly gifted child and her success in the role, at the age of 16, was immediate and wonderful, but the privations which came with the outbreak of war, the closing of the Opéra, and the siege of Paris, undermined her health and she died of smallpox on the morning of her 17th birthday, 23 November 1870. St Léon the choreographer had already died of exhaustion two months before, and before peace was to come to Paris, Dauty, the original Dr Coppélius had also died. Nevertheless, the delights of the story and the splendour of Delibes' score had earned *Coppélia* a place in the ballet repertory, and it continues to enchant audiences today as it has done for the past 100 years. It is notable also for the fact of the inclusion of folk dances as a major part of the choreography – one of St Léon's important innovations in the ballet of his time.

The Story of
COPPELIA

Coppélia, which had its first performance at the Paris Opéra in 1870, is the story of Swanilda, a peasant girl in Galicia, now part of Poland. Swanilda loves Frantz, but he is intrigued by a beautiful young woman whom he glimpses inside the house of Doctor Coppélius, an old scientist. In Act 1 Swanilda and Frantz quarrel over Frantz' flirtations. Dr Coppelius emerges from his house to take a glass of wine at the nearby inn, where he is teased and then jostled by the local lads, and inadvertently drops the key of his house. Swanilda and her girl friends find it, and decide that they must explore the mysterious house and visit the intriguing girl whom they have seen seated at the window. As they go in, Frantz also appears, bearing a ladder with which he hopes to enter the upper floor of the house to pay his respects to this same unknown beauty. Dr Coppélius, discovering the loss of his key, now returns to find his front door open, and as the curtain falls he goes in pursuit of the unknown intruders.

Act 2 takes place in Coppélius' workshop. Swanilda and her friends enter to be mystified and alarmed by strange beings dressed in exotic clothes. They are amazed and then amused to find that these are mechanical dolls, and even more amused when eventually they realize that the young girl whom they have all seen at the window is also an automaton, a life-sized doll. At this moment Dr Coppélius roars in and drives them all from his house. Or so he thinks; but Swanilda had taken refuge in the alcove where the doll, Coppélia, is hidden. No sooner has Coppélius recovered his breath, than Frantz steals into the room in search of the unknown charmer. Coppélius confronts him, and learning of the reason for this intrusion, is seized with an idea. He offers Frantz some drugged wine, and then prepares a magical experiment in which he will transfer the life-force from Frantz to the doll Coppélia. His fantastic dream of creating life can thus be realized. He wheels the doll from its alcove, not realizing that in fact Swanilda has changed places with it. As Coppélius casts his spells, it seems to him that the doll has become imbued with life. His delight increases as she dances for him, but Swanilda is determined to rescue Frantz so she teases and annoys the old man, and eventually succeeds in rousing Frantz. Together they mock Coppélius, show him the still inanimate figure of Coppélia, and run from the house, leaving Coppélius heart-broken.

Act 3 shows us the village's annual Festival of the Bell, at which betrothed couples are given a dowry. As Swanilda and Frantz, now completely reconciled, receive their money, the enraged Coppélius demands recompense; he is bought off, and the greater part of the act is devoted to dances of rejoicing.

Right Natalya Makarova in the *Don Quixote* pas de deux. Makarova always enjoys herself in the *Don Quixote* pas de deux, and communicates this enjoyment to her audience.

Left Roland Petit and Karen Kain in *Coppélia* with the Ballets de Marseille. In 1975 Roland Petit made a fascinating new version of this ballet in which he rethought the basic relationships in *Coppélia*. In witty French manner he imagined the three main characters to be part of the eternal triangle: Coppélius is in love with Swanilda who is in turn in love with Frantz who is in love with the doll Coppélia (which Coppélius has manufactured in the likeness of Swanilda). It is a sophisticated and typically sensitive dramatic idea from Petit, with a depth of feeling usually lacking in productions which stress the simple peasant quality of the tale. A notable fact of the staging was Roland Petit's own performance as Coppélius: no longer a doddering old scientist or a figure of fun, but an elegant man who is attracted to the pretty young Swanilda and who becomes a not unworthy rival for her hand. Petit's performance excited great enthusiasm, and Karen Kain – the Canadian ballerina who has danced in several roles for Petit's Marseille company – was an adorable and moving Swanilda.

Left Mikhail Barishnikov in the Kingdom of the Shades scene (Act 4) of *La Bayadère* with American Ballet Theatre. (See also next page.) *La Bayadère* was a four act ballet which Petipa staged in Petersburg in 1877 with a wildly complicated story involving Indian princes, a priest's daughter, and temple dancers, culminating in a splendid storm which brought a temple crashing in ruins and the death of everyone on stage. The ballet is still presented in a full (though slightly revised) version in Russia, and in Leningrad the staging makes use of a wonderful, life-size property elephant, but the gem of the ballet is the Kingdom of Shades scene. In it the hero, Solor, takes a drug and dreams that he is in the underworld, with his dead beloved Nikiya, surrounded by the ghosts of temple dancers (bayadères). It is a glorious display of the purest classical dancing, to be attempted only by a major company.

In 1963 Rudolf Nureyev restaged this scene for the Royal Ballet, and another eminent Leningrad artist, Natalya Makarova, made a production for American Ballet Theatre in 1975. It is this which we illustrate here, with Mikhail Barishnikov, yet another Leningrad star, in the role of Solor. Barishnikov (b 1948) was trained in Leningrad, and was the golden boy of the Kirov ballet. When still very young he was hailed by critics and audiences throughout the world as the most phenomenal dancer of his generation. In 1974, while on tour with a Soviet concert group in Canada, he decided to stay in the West, and since then he has danced a great deal with American Ballet Theatre, and has also appeared in many other countries. His dancing is distinguished for its classical purity and its breath-taking virtuosity, as well as for its dramatic intelligence. He is a unique and wonderful artist.

Despite the success of *Coppélia*, ballet was now losing its power to captivate audiences in the West. But in Russia it was entering upon its greatest period, thanks to Marius Petipa (1818–1910). Petipa was a member of yet another dancing family. His father Jean was a ballet-master, his brother Lucien was for years a principal dancer (he was the first Albrecht in *Giselle*) and later a choreographer at the Opéra. After many years dancing throughout Europe – and also making a disastrous trip to America in 1839 with his family – Marius Petipa was offered a post as principal dancer in St Petersburg in 1847, and apart from occasional visits to Paris, he was never to leave Russia again. He was the architect of the greatness of the Imperial Ballet in the last thirty years of the century, and it was the type of ballet which he developed in Petersburg, the grand evening-long spectacle in three, four or five acts, which was to set the pattern for the entertainments so loved by the court audience. It is important to realize that the ballet company and school were dependent upon the Tsar. The dancers could proudly claim to be 'Soloists to his Imperial Majesty' and when Petipa eventually assumed complete responsibility for the ballet in 1869, his instruction from the Director of the Imperial Theatres was to produce a new ballet every season. This Petipa contrived to do. His earliest success had been in 1862 when he composed *Pharaoh's Daughter*, an extravaganza in three acts, seven scenes, with prologue and epilogue, which established a formula of elaborate display based upon an improbable story. Thereafter Petipa produced an extraordinary succession of ballets of this type. They always contained complex set-pieces which showed off all the resources of a great company; there were processions, transformations, and most important, the culminating virtuoso variations for the ballerina and soloists.

The ballerina reigned supreme. In each act she had to have her solos (*variations*) or a pas de deux; her partner might also be allowed some moments of display, but the emphasis was still upon the female soloists, and their queen – the prima ballerina. Petipa was a craftsman of genius, and he planned his ballets with extreme care, providing his composer with an immensely detailed plan of the ballet's action to which the music had to be written. There existed in Russia at this time the official post of composer to the Imperial Ballet, a position which endured until the 1880s. Its last incumbent was Ludwig Minkus, composer of, among other ballets, *Don Quixote* and *La Bayadère*.

Below right Maya Plisetskaya in *Don Quixote*.
Marius Petipa first staged *Don Quixote* in
Moscow in 1869, reviving it for the Petersburg
Ballet a couple of years later. Despite its title
it has little to do with Cervantes' novel, apart
from a few brief scenes – for example, the
tilting with windmills. What it has a great deal
to do with, though, is dancing, and the version
which is seen nowadays provides a great
display of classical and character dancing.
The story is reduced to the love affair between
Kitri, a merry innkeeper's daughter, and Basil,
who is the town barber. Kitri's father wishes

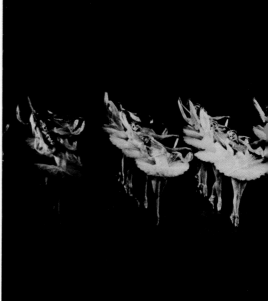

Above The corps de ballet of the Royal
Ballet in *La Bayadère*. In 1961 when the
Leningrad State Kirov Ballet first visited
London, the most fascinating work which
they brought with them was the Kingdom of
Shades scene from Petipa's *La Bayadère*.
Nothing could have prepared the audience for
the opening moment with its cumulative effect
of 32 dancers making their entrance in
arabesque penchée (see chapter five) down
a ramp, finally to fill the stage with glorious
dancing. This scene is one of the most
convincing examples of Petipa's ability to find
wonderful dance images that are still exciting
after 100 years.

Left Natalya Makarova and Mikhail
Barishnikov in the celebrated pas de deux
which is the culmination of the third act of
Don Quixote. It is most usually seen as a
concert item or as an isolated show-stopper
at galas – and this picture from BBC TV shows
just such an occasion, when Makarova and
Barishnikov fizzed through the pas de deux
for a televised Gala Performance from the
stage of the Sadler's Wells Theatre. It would
be difficult to find two artists better suited to
dance this show-piece. Their style and their
thrilling technique bring elegance as well as
exultant virtuosity to a duet which can
sometimes come dangerously close to a
circus act.

her to marry an absurd fop; but true love triumphs, in part, through the intervention of Don Quixote himself. Here Maya Plisetskaya as Kitri and Alexander Begak as Basil dance in Act 1 with the Bolshoy Ballet. Plisetskaya was like a blaze of fireworks in this scene when she danced it in London; in variations with fan, tambourine, and castanets she seemed the spirit of joy. Her virtuosity, the exultant brilliance of her dancing as she soared high over the stage, the wonderful charm of every moment of the performance, were unforgettable.

The whole aim of Petipa's ballets was brilliant display – cohorts of dancers were employed, and the dramatic sense of the story was less important than the opportunities it offered for all the elements that Petipa wished to include on stage. In a country rich in national dances, it was natural for each ballet to show some of these national elements under some pretext or another – either Slavic, or when necessary, Spanish and Italian. Petipa was ingenious in arranging scenes in which the ranks of the corps de ballet could be revealed – a fine example of this is the entry of the Shades in *La Bayadère*. He sometimes found the inspiration for his ballets in current events: *Pharaoh's Daughter* had been sparked by the enthusiasm at that time for Egyptian excavations; his *Roxana, the Beauty of Montenegro* saw the stage at the time of the Russian war with Turkey in the Balkans. But whatever the initial idea, the resultant ballet adhered to the formula of splendid display which he hoped would please his aristocratic court audience.

Although his ballets must have seemed repetitious there was a continuous development in dance technique, and the members of the Imperial Ballet were superbly trained artists. Nevertheless, star ballerinas were still imported to take the leading roles in many ballets, usually from Italy, where, although the ballets performed were undistinguished, the training – notably in Milan – produced dancers of exceptional virtuosity. One very important Italian visitor was Virginia Zucchi who arrived in Petersburg in 1885 to appear in a small theatre during the summer. Her technique excited admiration, but what gripped the public most was her extraordinary dramatic power. She was invited to appear with the Imperial Ballet and made a triumphant début in *Pharaoh's Daughter* and in Perrot's *La Esmeralda*. Her acting ability thrilled the Petersburg audiences who had been losing interest in ballet, and it is thanks to her performances that the public renewed its enthusiasm for the dance.

Zucchi's warm, vivid dramatic style was in direct contrast to the traditional mime gestures which were used to further the narrative in ballet. Some of this gesturing was easy to understand – a pointing finger, a hand raised to pledge an oath, a shaken fist, were quite comprehensible. Others might well be in code: hands circled above the head meant 'let us dance' and the arms extended and then crossed at the waist meant 'Die'. (In the second act of *Swan Lake*, Odette the enchanted Swan Queen relates her story to Prince Siegfried in mime gestures like these, and audiences today can hardly be expected to realize that Odette is standing beside a lake made of her mother's tears, which is what certain of her beautiful gestures are intended to signify.

The Italian invasion of the Imperial Theatre continued in 1890 when two virtuoso dancers, Carlotta Brianza and Enrico Cecchetti, were featured in *The Sleeping Beauty*. This masterpiece owes much to the then director of the Theatres, Ivan Alexandrovich Vsevolozhsky. He had invited Tchaikovsky to compose a score for the Maryinsky Theatre (which became the home of the ballet in Petersburg). Working to one of Petipa's elaborately detailed scenarios, Tchaikovsky matched every instruction with glorious music, and in 1890 *The Sleeping Beauty* was given its first performance. This was a typical 'fairy-ballet' of the time, based upon Perrault's fairy tale, with its underlying theme of good versus evil. (See following page for the story of this ballet.)

The Sleeping Beauty is the supreme example of the 'classic' ballet: the apotheosis of Petipa's career. It is the most difficult of the 19th century ballets to perform, demanding an army of classic dancers of the finest style and training, and the resources of a great opera house to stage it. Anything less must inevitably make the ballet look second-rate, and does great injustice to the geniuses who created it. Two years after *Beauty* Vsevolozhsky sought

Right Natalya Makarova and Mikhail Barishnikov in the last act pas de deux from *The Sleeping Beauty* in the production mounted by American Ballet Theatre in 1976. The final pas de deux of *The Sleeping Beauty* is the culmination of the whole ballet, and also of classic dance in the 19th century. It is noble, grand and brilliant, and it demands the most beautiful serenity and elegance of style. It must be presented with complete authority and a total absence of mannerism or affectation: the cavalier has to display his ballerina with dignity; the ballerina must seem absolutely poised and assured. For Makarova and Barishnikov these qualities are in-bred, part of their Leningrad inheritance, and they are ideal interpreters of the roles.

Left Irina Kolpakova in *The Sleeping Beauty* Act 1. Since its first performance there in 1890 *The Sleeping Beauty* has been permanently in the repertory in Leningrad. The same stage has seen generations of Auroras dance in this the greatest classical ballet of the 19th century. Irina Kolpakova, who is shown here in the dance in Act 1 when Aurora meets the four Princes who are suitors for her hand, is one of the very greatest interpreters of the role. A pupil of A. Y. Vaganova, Kolpakova's dancing seems the very essence of the most aristocratic classicism; that rare quality of perfect schooling is allied to an ideal physique and an absolute technical authority and serenity of manner. From her very first entrance Aurora is faced with one of the most taxing scenes in all ballets: the adagio in which the four princes present her with roses, culminating in a series of balances on point.

Below A hundred years after the spell has been cast and the court put to sleep, Prince Florimund is discovered on a hunting party in a forest. The Lilac Fairy appears, and shows him the vision of Princess Aurora. Florimund is fascinated by her beauty, and after dancing with the vision, he entreats the Lilac Fairy to lead him to the castle where Aurora sleeps. Here Antoinette Sibley and Anthony Dowell, a famous Royal Ballet partnership, are seen in the production of *The Sleeping Beauty* mounted by Kenneth MacMillan at the Royal Opera House in 1973.

The Story of
THE SLEEPING BEAUTY

The ballet starts with a prologue in which we see the christening of the infant Aurora. The fairy Godmothers invited by her father, King Florestan, have just bestowed their gifts, when a peal of thunder announces the arrival of an unexpected and uninvited guest. This is Carabosse, a wicked fairy, who declares that she too will bestow a gift upon the infant. One day she will prick her finger and die. Fortunately one other Godmother, the Lilac Fairy, has not yet given her blessing, and although she cannot completely reverse Carabosse's spell, she can weaken it's power. Aurora will not die; she will fall asleep for 100 years, and then be woken by a prince.

In the first Act, the court is celebrating Aurora's coming of age: four princes have come to seek her hand in marriage, and after dancing with them in the celebrated Rose Adagio in which, each in turn, the princes offer her roses, Aurora is intrigued by an old woman who holds out a mysterious object – a spindle. She has never seen such a thing before (all sharp pointed objects had been banned by her father from the kingdom to avoid injury to Aurora). She dances delightedly with it, when suddenly she stops and sees that she has pricked her finger, and she dances on in delirium before collapsing to the ground. The old woman reveals herself to be Carabosse, and laughs gleefully as her spell takes effect. She disappears, and at the same moment the Lilac Fairy enters to keep her promise. She waves her wand, and the court falls asleep, and immediately a magical forest grows up to hide them. A hundred years later, Act 2 shows us a young Prince out hunting near this same forest. He is bored with the hunt and dismisses his entourage, and the Lilac Fairy now appears to him, showing him a vision of Aurora. The prince falls in love with her and gladly consents to go in search of her. He follows the Lilac Fairy to Aurora's palace, and awakens her with a kiss. The third Act is a divertissement to celebrate the wedding of Aurora and her Prince.

Above The Bluebirds: Wayne Sleep and Jennifer Jackson in Act 3 of *The Sleeping Beauty* with the Royal Ballet. The last act is a divertissement in celebration of the wedding of Aurora and Prince Florimund. Fairy-tale characters are invited to attend, and one of the most brilliant dances in this scene is the pas de deux for the Bluebird and Princess Florine. This sequence was created by Marius Petipa to show off the amazing virtuosity of the Italian dancer Enrico Cecchetti who had come to Petersburg in the 1880s and had astounded audiences by his prodigious

technical skill. Cecchetti was a product of the school of ballet in Milan, and he was also to appear in the first performances of *Beauty* as the wicked fairy Carabosse – a tribute to his powers as a mime artist. At this time (1890) Cecchetti was already 40 years old; he remained in Petersburg as a teacher for many years, and for a while was private teacher to Anna Pavlova. He was associated with the Diaghilev company as teacher, and opened a school in London in 1918. The importance of his teaching methods was recognized, and his system was noted down and has since

become the basis for the Cecchetti Society's work. The method embodies the traditions of the Milanese school of the 19th century, brought up to date and revised by a great and inspiring teacher. In 1923 he returned to Milan to take charge of the ballet school at the Teatro alla Scala, and he died in that city in 1928. He appeared with the Diaghilev ballet, notably as the charlatan in *Petrushka* and the shopkeeper in *Boutique Fantasque*, and in 1921 he celebrated 50 years on stage by a single appearance as Carabosse in Diaghilev's *The Sleeping Princess*.

The technical demands of the role of the Bluebird are many: it requires wonderful elevation and brilliance in beaten steps (see chapter five), in which the male dancer must seem to hover and soar over the ground rather than to touch it. Wayne Sleep is a worthy successor to Cecchetti in the effortless buoyancy of his performance with the Royal Ballet and Jennifer Jackson is a charming young soloist with the company. The point of the pas de deux, often missed, is that Princess Florine is trying to emulate the flight of the Bluebird.

Above Jennifer Penney and David Wall in the grand pas de deux from the last act of *The Sleeping Beauty* with the Royal Ballet. Jennifer Penney is one of the several Commonwealth dancers who have risen to fame with the Royal Ballet; David Wall, who initially made a great reputation in many leading roles with the Royal Ballet's touring group, is now a leader of the company at Covent Garden. His vivid presence and technical authority have allowed him to play a very wide range of roles, from classics to contemporary works, many of which have been created for him.

Left Rudolf Nureyev in a solo from the second act of *The Nutcracker* with the Royal Ballet. In Leningrad, where he was trained, Nureyev learnt a version of *The Nutcracker* by the Soviet choreographer Vassili Vainonen. This staging was famous for its interesting adaptation of the traditional story, and it survived for many years in Russia. Nureyev, universally known today as one of the greatest stars in ballet thanks to the quality of his dancing and to his tireless performance schedules throughout the world, gives a most beguiling and delightful interpretation of the Prince.

Right Ekaterina Maximova and Vladimir Vasiliev in the grand pas de deux from *The Nutcracker* Act 2, with the Bolshoy Ballet. Because the *Nutcracker* has such a feeble story, and because its music by Tchaikovsky is so beautiful and so well loved, there have been a multitude of stagings and revisions of the ballet since it was first performed. Each Christmas, when this ballet customarily features in the repertory of companies throughout the world, there seem to be more and more new versions. None of these has proved wholly satisfactory, but the production for the Bolshoy Ballet by its director Yury Grigorovich is a charming one, especially when it has Maximova and Vasiliev in the leading roles. These two stars of the Bolshoy (who are husband and wife) are artists who combine wonderful technical brilliance with great warmth of personality: they are loved wherever they dance. They are seen in the pas de deux at the end of the ballet when the heroine, in her dream, dances with the Nutcracker prince.

to repeat its success, by inviting Tchaikovsky to compose the score for *The Nutcracker*, which Petipa was to stage. Once more Tchaikovsky delivered a glorious score, written to Petipa's very detailed notes, but the story itself presented problems. The action was weak and uninteresting; the ballerina had but one grand pas de deux in the last act, and the characters were flimsy.

Petipa fell ill before the ballet was put into rehearsal, and it was his assistant, Lev Ivanov (1834–1901), who was entrusted with the choreography. Despite his talent, he could do little with Petipa's scenario, and the ballet was much disliked at its first performance. What has preserved it since then in repertories of ballet companies all round the world has been the splendour of Tchaikovsky's music and many producers have tried to make the action more interesting in order to give the ballet greater appeal to the public.

Top Rudolf Nureyev and Merle Park in the pas de deux in Act 2 of *The Nutcracker*. In 1968 Rudolf Nureyev mounted his version of *The Nutcracker* for the Royal Ballet at Covent Garden, after previously staging it for the Royal Swedish Ballet in 1967. Nureyev has tried to make the story less like a children's tale by giving it psychological overtones which help to explain some of the oddities of the ballet's action: most notably, he has combined the roles of The Nutcracker Prince and Drosselmeyer. With designs by Nicholas Georgiadis, the production has been very successful with audiences at Covent Garden.

Above Patricia Wilde and Conrad Ludlow in the finale of George Balanchine's *The Nutcracker* for the New York City Ballet. Since 1954 the New York City Ballet has been giving an annual Christmas season of *The Nutcracker*. Though there have been many changes in the production, Mr Balanchine has remained true to Tchaikovsky's music and to the Hoffmann children's tale that inspired it. As a child in Petersburg Mr Balanchine danced in the Maryinsky production; then at the age of 15

he danced the Nutcracker Prince and his affection for the ballet plainly dates from that time. The present production is decorated by Reuben Ter-Arutunian with costumes by Karinska.

Right London Festival Ballet's production of *The Nutcracker*. From its earliest years, Festival Ballet presented a version of *The Nutcracker* in which Alicia Markova was a Sugar Plum Fairy and Snow Queen of incredible elegance and lightness. (Markova had known the ballet from its first British production with the Vic Wells Ballet). Over the years Festival presented this ballet for Christmas seasons in London, but in 1976 it was finally replaced by a very successful new version by Ronald Hynd which turned back to the original Hoffmann children's story to make more sense of the dramatic action. With designs by Peter Docherty, this new *Nutcracker* also incorporates opportunities for child-performers in the Chinese dance of Act 2 as well as at the party in Act 1. Manelle Jaye as Clara and Terry Hayworth as Counsellor Drosselmeyer are watching the divertissement.

Ivanov was next to be associated with Tchaikovsky in 1894. Tchaikovsky had died from cholera the year before at the tragically early age of 53, and it was decided to stage a performance in his memory. Seventeen years earlier, in 1877, he had written a score for the Moscow ballet company. This had been a huge failure, and following two further stagings, equally unsuccessful, in Moscow, the ballet had been forgotten. Now it was remembered, and the second act was presented at the memorial performance in a version by Ivanov. This was *Swan Lake*. The success of the second act was followed by a revival of the entire ballet the next year, and in 1895 *Swan Lake* was performed at the Maryinsky Theatre, Petersburg. In 1877 the symphonic nature of the score had defeated the uninspired Moscow choreographers; now with Ivanov composing the two lake-side acts and Petipa supervising the production and choreographing the first and third acts the ballet achieved its proper success, although it is a far more romantic and truly tragic story than was usual by now in Russian ballet.

It is this 1895 version of *Swan Lake* that has since conquered the world, to become the most popular of all ballets. The beauty of Tchaikovsky's music, with its deeply lyrical melodies; the perfect realization of this music in Ivanov's choreography and in the brilliance of Petipa's dances; and the extraordinary challenge of the double role of Odette/Odile, are all part of *Swan Lake*'s enduring appeal to audiences throughout the world. The role of Odette/Odile was created for yet another visiting Italian virtuoso ballerina in Petersburg. She was the prodigious Pierina Legnani (1863–1923), and she is remembered especially – and unworthily – for one particular trick. This was the *fouetté*, a whipped turn performed on point, for which she had a remarkable facility. She had staggered audiences by performing these in several ballets previously, but in the third act of *Swan Lake* Petipa used them to real dramatic effect: Legnani turned 32 *fouettés* '*sur place*' (i.e. on one spot) to suggest how Odile has dazzled the bemused Siegfried. Since that time, nearly every ballerina taking over the role has felt the need to accept this challenge, although the

The Story of
SWAN LAKE

The first act of *Swan Lake* finds Prince Siegfried celebrating his 21st birthday with his friends. Their dances are interrupted by the arrival of Siegfried's mother who reminds him that his coming of age means that he must marry. Prospective fiancées are to be presented for his approval at a grand ball the next night. Siegfried is unhappy, he does not wish to marry yet, and to distract himself he sets off on a hunt. Act 2 is set at a lake-side, and when Siegfried and his companions arrive there they see a flight of swans, and Siegfried commands that he shall be allowed to shoot the first one. His companions leave and Siegfried is amazed to see the leading swan change into a beautiful woman as she lands by the lake. She tells him that she is Odette, Queen of a group of maidens who have been enchanted by the magician von Rothbart. By day they must live as swans; only at nightfall can they resume their human shape. Siegfried falls deeply in love with this graceful creature, and he is told that the enchantment can only be broken if he swears to love Odette and no other. Von Rothbart appears, aware that his spell may be broken, and menaces Siegfried, and as dawn breaks the maidens resume the form of swans.

Act 3 takes place on the following night. The court is assembled in a palace ball-room for the reception of prospective fiancées. Siegfried's mind is still filled with the image of Odette and he pays little attention to the young girls who are presented to him. Suddenly heralds announce the arrival of unexpected guests: it is von Rothbart in disguise as a nobleman, bringing with him his daughter Odile, who has taken on the appearance of Odette. Enraptured, Siegfried dances with her, and Odile, prompted by von Rothbart, so bewitches him that he asks for her hand in marriage and swears to be true. With devilish glee von Rotherbart and Odile reveal themselves in their true colours and the figure of Odette is seen grieving at the palace window. She has been betrayed: she can never be released from her enchantment.

Act 4 finds the swans at the lake-side awaiting Odette, who appears lamenting Siegfried's unwitting treachery. When Siegfried himself comes to beg for Odette's forgiveness, she tells him that their only solution is to destroy themselves in the lake. Fleeing from von Rothbart, Odette and Siegfried both plunge into the waters of the lake. Their sacrifice ends the enchanter's powers, and he falls dead and the rest of the swan maidens are restored to human form as Siegfried and Odette are united.

Above Swan Maidens beginning the famous waltz in the second act of *Swan Lake* as presented by the Royal Ballet at Covent Garden. One of the best ways of judging a ballet company is on the quality of its corps de ballet, and like all the classics, *Swan Lake* reveals either the strength or the weakness of the company's artists. Great dancers are more numerous than great corps de ballet: unity of style, expressiveness and a sense of artistry are the qualities necessary, and they are admirably displayed by the corps of the Leningrad Kirov Ballet and the Royal Ballet.

Left Natalya Bessmertnova and Alexander Godunov in the pas de deux from Act 2 of *Swan Lake* with the Bolshoy Ballet. This pas de deux is one of the best known, best loved, and least understood moments in all ballet. With outstanding interpreters it becomes not only a superbly beautiful dance but also a passage of intense emotion and drama: Odette and Siegfried declare their love, and for the first time the tragic swan queen feels that she may be released from the cruel spell under which she is suffering. The dance calls for impeccable technique, lyricism, musicality and the ability to express poetic ideas without strain or mannerism.

Right One of the great Swan Queens of our time has been Dame Margot Fonteyn, whose supremacy in the classic repertory did much to help British audiences' understanding of the old ballets. She is seen here in Act 2 in a picture taken during the 1950s with Michael Somes as Siegfried on the right, and Bryan Ashbridge as Benno — a character who no longer features in current stagings of *Swan Lake*. Michael Somes, a dancer of great nobility, was Dame Margot's partner for several years after the war.

Left Natalya Makarova in Act 3 of *Swan Lake* with the Royal Ballet. Traditionally known as the *Black Swan*, this part of the third act introduces Odile, the sorcerer von Rothbart's daughter who tries to beguile Siegfried into betraying his pledge to love Odette. It is a celebrated virtuoso show-piece, with the famous 32 *fouettés* at its culmination. The double role of Odette/Odile presents a ballerina with the massive challenge of dancing in the lake-side scenes with purest lyricism, and then dancing in Act 3 with extreme virtuosity which must also make dramatic sense as Odile tries to dazzle Siegfried into believing that she is the Odette to whom he has pledged his love. Natalya Makarova is seen in an action shot taken during a Royal Ballet's visit to New York: the excitement and intensity of her performance are very well caught in this exultant pose.

Below Dame Margot Fonteyn in *Raymonda* Act 1 with the Australian Ballet. Although this ballet, staged in Petersburg in 1898, has been regularly performed in Russia, it is thanks to Rudolf Nureyev that post-war audiences have been able to see this ballet in the West. He has staged it, and starred in it, with the Zurich Ballet, American Ballet Theatre and the Australian Ballet. Although, like *La Bayadère*, its plot is all but nonsensical, the beauty of its score by Alexander Glazunov, and much of Petipa's choreography, have ensured its preservation. Here Dame Margot Fonteyn is seen in a beautiful *attitude* (see chapter five), which shows her excellent classical line and the radiance of manner which has made her adored throughout the world; these qualities have always been the hall-mark of her performances wherever she has danced.

ability to turn *fouettés* is not the criterion for a good Odette/Odile. The really necessary qualities of lyric intensity and dramatic power are rarely found, and today the role, like that of Giselle or Aurora is too frequently danced by ballerinas who are ill-suited to it.

Although Marius Petipa was by now an old man, his control over the Imperial Ballet was still absolute and his creativity unimpaired. In 1898 he staged his last important three act ballet in St Petersburg. This was *Raymonda*, and once again he had a magnificent score from the young Alexander Glazunov, who was recognized as a natural successor to Tchaikovsky in producing grand and danceable music. Alas, the ballet was hampered by a very silly libretto. Briefly, *Raymonda* tells of a young girl in medieval Provence who is awaiting the return of her beloved, Jean de Brienne, from the Crusades. A Saracen warrior, Abdérâme, arrives and tries to abduct her, but Jean turns up just in time, and defeats the Saracen in combat. The third act of the ballet was a grand Hungarian divertissement (the unlikeliness of its being Hungarian was explained by having King Andrew II of Hungary as a friend of Jean) in which the happy couple were reunited. The ballet is still performed, most usually in Russia, thanks to the beauty of the Glazunov score and the intricacy of Petipa's dances, and it has been recently revived in the West in versions arranged by Rudolf Nureyev for several companies. Petipa continued to produce further ballets, but in 1903, following the failure of his last full-length work – *The Magic Mirror* – he was finally forced to retire, and the Imperial Ballet in Petersburg lost the creative impetus that had sustained it during his reign. The ballet school continued to produce magnificent artists: the example of the Italian virtuoso dancers had been absorbed and now the Russian dancers were the finest in the world. Their style combined the French school of Auguste Vestris (brought to Russia by Jules Perrot and several later ballet-masters), Italian brilliance and native Russian fire, but there was no new choreographic talent to utilise this tremendous reservoir of talent. There was a good deal of dissatisfaction among the more serious artists of the company, and the next important development in Russian ballet took place far away from Russia. This was the Diaghilev Ballet Russe.

DIAGHILEV AND THE BALLET RUSSE

One of the soloists in the first performance of *Raymonda* was an eighteen-year-old dancer, Mikhail Fokine, for whom great things were forecast. He was amongst those artists who were profoundly discontented with the stultified atmosphere of the Imperial Ballet at the beginning of the new century. This discontent was heightened by the great changes in art that were happening at the turn of the century, and also by the feeling of political instability that came to a head in the abortive revolution of 1905 in Russia. Fokine believed that ballet must achieve a greater naturalness – like Noverre in the 18th century he was eager for a return to a true and dramatic expressiveness in dancing. His very earliest choreography aimed for this; in 1905 he composed a simple and beautiful solo, *The Dying Swan*, for one of the most outstanding young ballerinas in Petersburg, Anna Pavlova. But it was his first ballet staged at the Maryinsky Theatre, *Le Pavillon d'Armide*, which really revealed his gifts. He had to fight to have it put on, and the management were so uninterested that the ballet was eventually presented at the end of a programme that had already contained the whole of *Swan Lake*. Nevertheless, it was a great success, and had brought Fokine into contact with an exceptional figure of the time, the painter Alexandre Benois (1870–1960), who was responsible for the decor. Through Benois he was also introduced into the circle which surrounded a young amateur, Serge Diaghilev.

Diaghilev (1872–1929) had already at this time edited an influential art magazine, and presented a series of very important exhibitions of paintings in St Petersburg. He had also been employed for a brief period by the director of the Imperial Theatres but his adventurous ideas were not at all to the taste of the very conservative and unbending administration of the ballet. Diaghilev had plainly been searching for a proper outlet for his talents, and after organizing exhibitions, concerts and opera performances in Paris between 1906 and 1908 to show the West some of the glories of the arts in Russia, he had decided to present some of the great dancers of the Imperial Theatre in Petersburg and Moscow in a combined opera and ballet season in 1909. From this season sprang the rebirth of ballet in the Western world. Diaghilev's enterprise was an explosion of all the arts of which ballet is composed, and in the 20 years from 1909 until 1929 when Diaghilev died, the greatest creative artists of Europe worked for Diaghilev's Russian Ballet (usually known by its French title: Ballet Russe). Diaghilev's genius lay in his ability to combine the talents of others, to inspire them, guide them, coerce, coax, threaten and charm them, and give them the opportunities to develop. He had an uncanny ability to detect young talent, and his entire career was spent in the search for the new and exciting directions for ballet and its associated arts. The first two seasons of the Ballet Russe were short visits abroad when the dancers were on holiday from the Imperial Theatres in Petersburg and Moscow. Despite the brevity of their visits, the impact on the West was enormous: Paris and a few other important cities had never before seen such superbly gifted dancers, nor such theatrical excitement associated with dancing. It was the ballets of Mikhail Fokine which made up the repertory – Diaghilev's aims and those of Fokine were identical in achieving a union between dance, drama, music and design. Performers like Anna Pavlova, Tamara Karsavina, Vaslav Nijinsky and Adolf Bolm, were a revelation to the new public, as were the designs of Benois and Léon Bakst, and the music of the Russian composers, and especially of Diaghilev's first great discovery, Igor Stravinsky.

By 1911, Diaghilev had formed a permanent company. Nijinsky had been fired by the Imperial Ballet following a disagreement about his costume in *Giselle* which had offended

Chopiniana (*Les Sylphides*) as staged at the Bolshoy Theatre, Moscow. Mikhail Fokine first created his suite of dances to Chopin's music as an evocation of the romantic period of Taglioni for his pupils at the Imperial Ballet School in Petersburg. Since then it has been preserved in Russia under its original title of *Chopiniana*. When Diaghilev took the ballet to Paris for the very first season of the *Ballet Russe*, he decided to rename it *Les Sylphides* and under this name it is widely performed throughout the world.

the Dowager Empress, during a performance at the Maryinsky Theatre and Diaghilev seized this opportunity to form a troupe which would tour throughout the West. Pavlova had left him after the first season in order to devote herself to travelling the world with her own company, but Diaghilev engaged some of the finest artists from Petersburg and Moscow, with Karsavina as his ballerina, Fokine as chief choreographer, and Benois and Bakst as his associates.

In the first three years, a magnificent roster of ballets had already been mounted. All were by Fokine. A work which he had first made for the students of the Imperial Ballet School in Petersburg – *Chopiniana* – was brought to Paris in 1909, and renamed *Les Sylphides*, since it paid homage to the era of the Romantic ballet and the ethereal grace of Marie Taglioni. Even more exciting to the audience in that first season had been the barbaric fury of the Polovtsian warriors in *Prince Igor*; in this the virility of Adolf Bolm as the Polovtsian chief, and the incredible leaps and dramatic skill of Nijinsky in other ballets had reminded audiences of the forgotten possibilities of male dancing. Pavlova and Karsavina were no less exciting to audiences, and in Diaghilev's second season in Paris in 1910, two new ballets by Fokine were to create a sensation. *Firebird*, with its fairy-tale story, was a herald of the new music that Stravinsky was to compose over the next few years; *Schéhérazade*, an oriental fantasy, dazzled the public with its exotic sensuality and its glowing colours. In these two ballets vastly important developments in music and stage design had taken place. In the following year a ballet was produced which is still recognized as the finest achievement of the whole Diaghilev era. This was *Petrushka*.

Left Vaslav Nijinsky as the Golden Slave in *Scheherazade*. The most legendary figure in the whole history of ballet is Nijinsky. Despite a tragically short career (he danced for only 10 years and retired from the stage at the age of 29), he is remembered wherever ballet is known. Although he danced classic roles in Petersburg and with Diaghilev, he is most associated with those 'exotic' parts which were made for him: Petrushka, The Golden Slave, The Spectre of the Rose, his own Faun, and the Poet in *Les Sylphides*. This photograph, taken during the Ballet Russe's first visit to London in 1911, indicates, despite the 'dated' costume, the extraordinary physical presence that he emanated even in a posed studio photograph.

Top Tamara Karsavina in *Les Sylphides* – a photograph taken in Berlin during one of the early visits of the Diaghilev Ballet. In this exquisite arabesque Karsavina seems to defy the laws of gravity and some impression can be gained of the beauty of a ballerina who was an inspiration to generations of audiences and dancers alike.

Opposite right Anna Pavlova in *Paquita* – a photograph taken in Germany before the First World War. *Paquita* was a two act ballet dating from 1846 which was preserved in the repertory in Petersburg as a tremendous display-piece, and its most famous section, the *grand pas*, is still danced in Leningrad. This photograph conveys something of Pavlova's extraordinary charm and gives a good idea of her exquisite feet.

Opposite below Serge Diaghilev and Serge Lifar – a photograph taken at a railway station in 1927. Lifar is holding a coconut, perhaps due to his appearances in *Petrushka*, in which the Blackamoor dances with a coconut.

Right The Dying Swan. This brief solo is forever associated with Anna Pavlova. Mikhail Fokine composed it for her in 1905 during one rehearsal. Pavlova had asked him for a solo that she could perform at a gala evening, and Fokine, who had been playing Saint-Saëns' music on a mandoline, realized that the music and the dancer were ideally suited to each other. 'It was almost an improvisation. I danced in front of her, she directly behind me. Then she danced and I walked alongside her, curving her arms, and correcting details of poses.' Thus wrote Fokine, and he later said to the distinguished English critic Arnold Haskell: 'It is a dance of the whole body and not of the limbs only, it appeals not merely to the eye but to the emotions and the imagination.'

Anna Pavlova performed *The Dying Swan* throughout her career, which ended in 1931 in the Hague, where she died of pneumonia.

Many ballerinas since Pavlova have attempted this solo, giving a variety of different interpretations to the simple-seeming steps. The dance is in fact based upon the *pas de bourrée* (a sequence of small travelling steps on point), and in the hands of anyone less than a great artist can seem sentimental. Plisetskaya is shown here in her dramatic and very moving realization of Pavlova's dance.

Right Les Sylphides as staged for London Festival Ballet by Dame Alicia Markova in 1976. *Les Sylphides*, even though it is performed throughout the world and is immensely popular with audiences, is a most difficult ballet to dance correctly. Fokine himself said that there is no corps de ballet: every dancer in it is a soloist. It is the particular distinction of Dame Alicia Markova that she studied the ballet, and especially its three principal roles – the ballerinas of the waltz, of the mazurka and of the prelude – with Fokine. Throughout her career she was an ideal interpreter of the great romantic and classic ballets, and her reconstruction of *Les Sylphides* for London Festival Ballet is marked by her wonderful understanding of its style and the nuances that give it its choreographic meaning. Fokine described the work as a romantic reverie – in Markova's staging, this quality is beautifully preserved.

Left *The Three Cornered Hat*. London Festival Ballet has been at pains to preserve several of the finest ballets of the Diaghilev period in its repertory, and among the most important is Leonid Massine's *The Three Cornered Hat*. This was created as a direct result of Diaghilev's time in Spain during the First World War. While part of his company was performing in South America, Diaghilev and Massine undertook a long tour through Spain with the Spanish composer Manuel de Falla, acting as their guide. They were also accompanied by a brilliant young gypsy dancer, Felix, who was able to introduce them to the dances of his country. The result of this immersion in the music and dance of Spain was the decision to stage *The Three Cornered Hat*. First performed in London in 1919, when the Diaghilev troupe had been rescued from its war-time troubles, De Falla's score made use of melodies which he had heard played by street musicians. The choice of Picasso for the design was a natural one, and his feeling for his native land was translated into deceptively simple décor of great atmospheric power. The picture shows the last scene in the ballet, an exciting *Jota* for the whole cast in which an effigy of the ridiculous Corregidor (the regional governor of a district who wears the three cornered hat of the title) is tossed in a blanket, to show the villagers' contempt for the old man who has tried to seduce the local miller's wife.

Right Design by Léon Bakst for King Florestan in *The Sleeping Princess*. Léon Bakst (1866–1924) was a member of Diaghilev's close circle of friends in Petersburg who were to become his associates in the creation of the Ballet Russe. Together with Alexandre Benois, Bakst was responsible for most of the designing during the early seasons of the Diaghilev enterprise. His almost barbaric sense of colour, and his consummate skill in evoking exotic and mysterious settings, mark him as one of the greatest stage designers of all time. The impact of his designs was tremendous; they even influenced women's clothes and the interior decoration of homes for more than a decade. In 1916 he provided the decoration for a Broadway season by Anna Pavlova in which she danced some scenes from *The Sleeping Beauty*, but it was in 1921 that Bakst placed his unforgettable imprint upon the work. Diaghilev revived it for a season in London, and Bakst's designs were a superlative evocation of the French court in the late 17th century.

Left London Festival Ballet in the last scene of *Petrushka*. The inspiration for the setting of *Petrushka* was the Butter-week Fair held during Lent in Petersburg in 1840, and the designs of Alexandre Benois are a marvellous evocation of this scene. Benois, Fokine and Stravinsky worked in the closest association during the composition of this masterpiece, and design, dance and music merge into an artistic unity which was the hallmark of Diaghilev's work. We see here the coachmen's dance in the fourth scene of the ballet: the vivid activity of the crowd and the bustle and excitement of the fair are an essential part of the action.

Its three creators, Fokine, Benois and Stravinsky, worked in ideally close collaboration, under the all-seeing eye of Diaghilev, and the part of the tragic puppet, Petrushka, provided Nijinsky with what was probably his greatest role. Nijinsky (1888–1950), a unique performer, had captured the imagination even of people who never saw him. His gift for total identification with a role, and his power to compel the audience's belief in him, was quite as remarkable as his prodigious technical feats, with his seeming ability to hover in the air at the height of one of his phenomenal jumps.

Although audiences were clamouring for ballets that were already their favourites, Diaghilev was insistent upon finding new creators and new ideas for ballets. In 1912 he encouraged Nijinsky to make his first choreography. This was *L'Après-midi d'un faune* (with music by Debussy), a revolutionary ballet in that it rejected every rule of turn-out and classical presentation of the body. Instead, Nijinsky showed a faun and 6 nymphs moving in choreography that was almost entirely walking steps performed on a single plane – to give the effect of a classical frieze. Audiences were unprepared for this new style, and for what they took to be an indecent gesture at the close of the ballet, but nevertheless Diaghilev continued to encourage Nijinsky. So much so that Fokine quit the company in a huff, and Diaghilev now had to rely upon the 23-year-old Nijinsky as choreographer and principal dancer. In 1913 Nijinsky staged two further ballets – *Jeux*, a mysterious piece about three tennis players, to a shimmering Debussy score – and *The Rite of Spring*. This boasted Stravinsky's most monumental and adventurous score to date, and the seeming harshness of the music and the primitive movements of the dancers brought about a celebrated riot in the theatre at the first performance in Paris, during which the audience hurled abuse at the dancers and at each other, and soon started fighting among themselves as the dancers endeavoured to perform the very complex choreography.

This same year was to show the eclipse of Nijinsky. He married, and this infuriated Diaghilev, who dismissed him from the company. Although Nijinsky returned briefly to the Ballet Russe during the war for some performances in North and South America, he became increasingly mentally disturbed and in 1917 he danced for the last time. Within a year he had been committed to a sanatorium in Switzerland, and the last three decades of his life – he died in 1950 – were spent in the shadows of mental ill-health. Diaghilev, however, soon found a new young talent in Leonid Massine (born in 1895). A dancer with the Moscow Bolshoy ballet, Massine joined Diaghilev in 1914, and during the war – when Diaghilev remained in Western Europe and struggled to keep his company together – Massine proved to be both an exceptional character dancer, and, which was more important, a most gifted choreographer. When the Ballet Russe returned to London to start its first post-war season in 1918, it was two new Massine works which provided the fresh excitement always associated with Diaghilev. These were *The Three Cornered Hat* and *La Boutique Fantasque*.

But the 1920s were not always to be a happy time for the Ballet Russe. Financial problems, which had constantly beset the Diaghilev enterprise, grew worse. His greatest financial disaster came during the 1921–22 season in London with the glorious re-staging of *The Sleeping Princess* (Diaghilev preferred this title to the more usual *Sleeping Beauty*) magnificently decorated by Léon Bakst. Without a choreographer (Massine had left the company) Diaghilev hoped that a revival of the greatest of all classical ballets would capture the interest of the public. Alas this did not prove to be so: Diaghilev had taught his public to want short, entertaining ballets, and the classic grandeur of Imperial Russia – and the superlative casts – were beyond the audience's comprehension.

From the financial disaster that came with *The Sleeping Princess*, though artistically it was a triumph, Diaghilev found a new choreographer, who matched the mood of the 1920s. This was Nijinsky's sister, Bronislava Nijinska (1891–1972). She had appeared with the Ballet Russe before the war, and had been re-engaged for *The Sleeping Princess* as dancer and to provide some additional choreography. Now she produced two very important works for Diaghilev: *Les Biches* and *Les Noces*. When Nijinska, in her turn, left Diaghilev, she was eventually to be replaced by a young dancer who had come out of Soviet Russia in 1924. George Balanchine was a product of the great school in Petersburg (also called Petrograd; later to be renamed Leningrad). With three other dancers, he

Top left Dudley von Loggenburg and Manola Asensio in *Schéhérazade* with London Festival Ballet. The story of *Schéhérazade*, an Arabian Night's tale of passion, slaves and drama in a harem, is faintly silly. What makes this early Diaghilev ballet so exciting in the theatre today is the beauty of the sets and costumes by Léon Bakst, and the conviction with which dancers like Dudley von Loggenburg and Manola Asensio play their roles. Manola Asensio is Zobeide, Queen of the harem; Dudley von Loggenburg is the Golden Slave who is her lover.

Below left David Wall as Ivan Tsarevich in *The Firebird* with the Royal Ballet at one of the dramatic moments in Fokine's early master-piece. The hero, Ivan Tsarevich, is holding aloft the feather from the magic Firebird which will allow him to destroy the power of the evil wizard Kastchey, seen on the right. Behind them are some of the monsters in Kastchey's court.

Top right *Les Noces*. Igor Stravinsky's early scores for Diaghilev had become world famous and he wrote *Les Noces* while living in Switzerland during the First World War. It

is a work that evokes the feelings of a Russian peasant wedding and when Diaghilev heard the music it is reported that he wept at its nostalgic power. But it was not until 1923 that the music was used for a ballet, when Bronislava Nijinska staged it for the Ballet Russe. Her choreography is unique in its simplicity and strength, and uses massed groups of dancers: the austere designs by Natalya Goncharova are complementary in their avoidance of unnecessary decoration.

In 1966 Sir Frederick Ashton, then Director of the Royal Ballet, invited Mme Nijinska to mount the work at Covent Garden, thus paying tribute to a woman whose work had had a great influence upon him as a young choreographer. Here is one of the characteristic groups in the choreography, with Svetlana Beriosova as the Bride. *Les Noces* is an extremely difficult ballet to perform, with complicated rhythms for the dancers to interpret.

Below right Vyvyan Lorrayne as the siren in *Prodigal Son* with the Sadler's Wells Royal Ballet. It is the Siren who is to bring about the downfall and degradation of the Prodigal Son and Vyvyan Lorrayne is a fine interpreter of the role.

Above Parade. It was typical of Diaghilev that, during the First World War when his company was surviving with the greatest difficulty, he should be able to produce a work as daring and controversial as *Parade* (first staged in 1917). Every element in it was adventurous. The theme was devised by the young French poet Jean Cocteau; the music was by the most eccentric French composer of the time, Erik Satie, and made use of ships' sirens and a typewriter in the score; the designs were by Pablo Picasso, his first work for the theatre, and featured the theories of the newest artistic movement of the time, Cubism. The choreography was by the 22-year-old Leonid Massine. The ballet is a series of dances designed to entice people into a theatre: (in French *Parade* means a kind of 'trailer' for an entertainment). Comic mannerisms of the stars of silent movies, the sinking of the

Titanic, and a pantomime horse were all incorporated in the choreography which is introduced to the audience by two grotesque figures representing a French and an American manager. These figures are dressed in weird constructions, which can be seen on either side of the illustration. Other characters shown are two acrobats, a Chinese conjuror, and the Little American Girl. The production is that which Leonid Massine made for London Festival Ballet in 1974.

Below The Prodigal Son was the last work staged by the Diaghilev Ballet. It was choreographed by George Balanchine in 1929 and tells the biblical story of the young man who leaves home and wastes his inheritance, finally returning repentant to his father. Diaghilev, typically, used two

important creators to complement the choreography: Georges Rouault, one of the greatest French painters of his time, designed the ballet and Sergey Prokofiev wrote the music. Prokofiev was to write several outstanding ballet scores both for Diaghilev and for ballet companies in his native Russia – notably *Romeo and Juliet*, *Cinderella* and *The Stone Flower*. The first interpreter of the Prodigal Son was Serge Lifar, and by all accounts he has never been surpassed, though in stagings for The Royal Ballet and for New York City Ballet there have been memorable performances by a number of male dancers. The illustration shows the New York City Ballet's production by Balanchine, with Edward Villella as the Prodigal and Karen von Aroldingen as the Siren in the banquet scene when the Prodigal is seduced and robbed by the Siren and her accomplices.

left Russia to embark upon a summer tour of the Baltic, and the quartet turned their backs on their homeland. They joined Diaghilev: one of the girls in the group, Alexandra Danilova was to become a great ballerina during the next 30 years; Balanchine was to become Diaghilev's last choreographer. For the Ballet Russe he composed several lightweight ballets, but with *Apollo* (1928) and *The Prodigal Son* (1929) he created two works that were vitally important.

During the post-war years, as during the whole of his career with the ballet, Diaghilev continued to engage the most important and adventurous painters and composers in Europe. Diaghilev and his circle were very influential in the artistic movements of the time, since their activities extended far beyond the bounds of ballet itself. When Diaghilev died in 1929, his company disbanded – as no other man was strong enough to hold together this extraordinary enterprise once the master was gone. The Diaghilev legacy is phenomenal: during the 20 years of the Ballet Russe's existence it had commissioned scores from Stravinsky, Ravel, Debussy, Prokofiev, Richard Strauss, Satie, Manuel de Falla, Poulenc, Milhaud; designs had been provided by Bakst, Benois, Picasso, Derain, Braque, Utrillo, Matisse, Tchelichev, Ernst, de Chirico, and Rouault, among others.

This list, which could be extended, is a roll-call of many of the greatest creators in Europe during the first part of the century. Diaghilev chose them, sometimes gave them their first chance to work in the theatre, brought them together to work for the great glory of ballet, and presented their work to a much wider public than might otherwise have known them. No one since has been able to come anywhere near rivalling Diaghilev's genius, which was hugely creative through other people's creativity.

Above Natalya Goncharova's design for *The Firebird*. For its first production in 1910 *The Firebird* was designed by Golovin, with costumes by Léon Bakst. In 1926 Diaghilev revived the ballet, with new sets and costumes from the distinguished Russian painter Natalya Goncharova (1881–1962) and the beautiful back-cloth which we illustrate was made for the final scene of the ballet – the wedding of the hero Ivan Tsarevich and the beautiful princess he had rescued from the enchantments of the evil Kastchey. Goncharova's stylized view of an ancient Russian city was perfectly suited to the folk-tale quality of the ballet.

The phenomenal quality of the designs for the Ballet Russe has already been emphasised. Never before, and never since, have so many of the world's finest artists worked for the ballet, and brought such visual distinction to the theatre. Diaghilev did a great deal to foster public interest in modern art. Today it is rare that a dance company asks fine easel painters to provide sets: the preference is to use specialized theatre designers.

Right Les Biches. Nijinska's next ballet for Diaghilev was totally different from *Les Noces*. This was *Les Biches* (a title almost untranslatable, though it literally means female deer). The ballet is a witty, wordly portrait of elegant life at a society house-party during the 1920s in the South of France. The décor by the fashionable painter Marie Laurencin is airy and charming in its use of pastel colours. Members of the house-party include a group of sweet young things in pink dresses, who are very amused by the appearance of a trio of young male athletes who have come in from the beach.

A central figure is the mysterious creature in a blue tunic, seen in the centre of the picture – a role magnificently taken by Georgina Parkinson with the Royal Ballet, whose staging this is. The ballet, although it reflects everything of the superficiality of society life in the 1920s, lives today because of the skill with which Nijinska constructed it, and because of the beauty of the score by Francis Poulenc and the delicacy of Laurencin's designs. Like *Les Noces*, it is difficult to perform well – but the Royal Ballet's staging, which was made by Mme Nijinska, is a very successful revival.

BALLET AND MODERN DANCE SINCE THE 1930s

Within two years of Diaghilev's death in 1929, the other great exponent of the dance, Anna Pavlova had also died. Between them, these two had created a world-wide enthusiasm for ballet. What Diaghilev had offered his public was entertainment employing the finest artistic resources of the time. Pavlova gave her devotees the experience of an incredible star performer, touring world-wide in cities and even townships totally unreachable by the grander Ballet Russe, thrilling audiences by the passionate intensity of her presence. Her influence was incalculable in inspiring a love of dance: in Lima, Peru, a small English boy saw her and determined to make his career as a dancer. He was Frederick Ashton, one of the architects of British ballet as we know it today.

After the dissolution of the Diaghilev and Pavlova companies, there was a vacuum. Just as the itinerant ballet-masters of Italy and France had spread the art of ballet throughout Europe in previous centuries, so now Diaghilev's choreographers and dancers transported their talents and ideas to the central cities of the Western world. During the 1930s the creation of important national ballet companies owed everything to Diaghilev's former artists. In Britain two remarkable women – Marie Rambert and Ninette de Valois – were responsible for the creation of two major companies. In Paris, the ballet at the Opéra had long been dormant. Now Serge Lifar, Diaghilev's last star male dancer, became ballet-master and principal dancer, and during the next quarter of a century he re-established the prestige of this oldest ballet company in Europe. In America several former Diaghilev dancers had settled as teachers and performers, but it was the arrival of Balanchine in 1933 which really marks the arrival of classical dance in the USA. In America at this time, there was another style of dancing, absolutely opposed to the classic ballet. This has become known as 'Modern Dance'. Its first great figure was Isadora Duncan who was born in San Francisco in 1878, and died in France in 1927. A great revolutionary of the dance, Duncan had made a sensational career in Europe. In recitals she had shown dancing free from toe-shoes, corsets, and all the artificialities of the classical ballet of the time. She had returned to ancient Greece for her inspiration, and her dances – performed to great music, even including symphonies – had been immensely influential. With no great technique but with a phenomenal star quality, Duncan seemed like the very spirit of freedom. Her life was often scandalous, and ultimately tragic, but she was a beacon to the world of the dance, proclaiming the glory of free movement to those who were dissatisfied with the strict confines of classical technique. Her example fired many imaginations, particularly in central Europe and in America. In her native land some of her ideas were taken up by Ruth St Denis (1877–1968) and Ted Shawn (1891–1972), whose company and schools established in Los Angeles and New York were in turn the nursery of the most influential choreographers and dancers of the Modern Dance in the 1930s and 1940s: notably Martha Graham (b 1893) and Doris Humphrey (1895–1958). From Graham and Humphrey and their contemporaries has, in turn, sprung the present magnificent generation of modern dancers and choreographers – such figures as Merce Cunningham, Paul Taylor, Twyla Tharp, and many, many more.

Brenda Last as Lise, Desmond Kelly as Colas, David Morse as Alain in the second scene of Sir Frederick Ashton's comic masterpiece, *La Fille Mal Gardée*, as staged by the Sadler's Wells Royal Ballet. *Fille* is one of the happiest of ballets, telling the story of how Lise manages to marry the boy she loves, Colas, and outwits her mother who wants her to marry the wealthy idiot, Alain. *Fille* is both a new and an old ballet. A first version was staged by Jean Dauberval in 1789 in Bordeaux. Various productions survived during the 19th century, but Sir Frederick Ashton made a brand new version in 1960, and since then it has enchanted the world. It is a ballet that is in the repertory of both halves of the Royal Ballet.

At the same time that important national companies were being formed in Britain and America, audience interest was being sustained in classic ballet by the revival of the Ballet Russe. In the early 1930s two impresarios, Col. W. de Basil and René Blum, re-assembled many of the ballets and stars of the Diaghilev company. The resulting Ballets Russes brought back to audiences round the world the glamour and excitement of 'The Russian Ballet'. Its main achievements were the new ballets created by Leonid Massine – notably his works set to symphonies by Brahms, Tchaikovsky, Beethoven and Berlioz – as well as delightfully light-hearted ballets like *Le Beau Danube* and *Gaieté Parisienne*. The stars, besides Massine, included Alexandra Danilova and in due course the exceptional English ballerina Alicia Markova (who had joined Diaghilev as a child in 1925). Blum and de Basil, like Diaghilev, also had their child stars. These were the three 'baby ballerinas': Tatiana Riabouchinska (b 1917), Tamara Toumanova (b 1919) and Irina Baronova (b 1919) who were discovered as very young students in the Paris dance studios being run at that time by former ballerinas of the Petersburg Imperial Ballet who had fled to France at the time of the Revolution. Baronova, Riabouchinska and Toumanova became internationally celebrated, and very fine dancers, at the age of 14 and 15, when their English contemporaries, for example, were still wearing plaits and worrying about results of hockey matches. Despite a good deal of managerial quarrelling – Blum and de Basil eventually separated and formed two distinct companies – the Ballets Russes were an essential part of ballet in the 1930s. Following the outbreak of the 1939 war, both companies were eventually to be found in America: de Basil's company returned to Europe after the war but did not long survive. Blum was a victim of Nazi persecution but his company continued in the USA under Serge Denham until the 1960s.

BRITAIN

Both Marie Rambert and Ninette de Valois served an important apprenticeship with Diaghilev. Marie Rambert, born in Warsaw in 1888, was invited to join the Diaghilev enterprise in 1912, to help Nijinsky in his work on the very difficult Stravinsky score for *Rite of Spring*. She came to London during the 1914–1918 war and married the English playwright Ashley Dukes, and thereafter settled in London where she opened a school. From this there developed a classical dance company, small in numbers but rich in talent. Amongst Rambert's pupils were two men who, in particular, were to become choreographers of international importance: Frederick Ashton (b 1904) and Antony Tudor (b 1909). During the 1930s Rambert's company, ever surviving on a shoe-string, created a repertoire which included several enduring masterpieces by Tudor – notably *Jardin aux Lilas* and *Dark Elegies* – and provided the first opportunities for several subsequently celebrated choreographers and dancers. Marie Rambert's gift for discovering and inspiring creative talent has been vital in the formation of British ballet.

Simultaneously, Ninette de Valois had also set to work. Of Anglo-Irish descent, born in 1898, de Valois had danced with Diaghilev during the 1920s and had then opened a school in London. She had dreams of an English national ballet, and the realization of these dreams owed much to another redoubtable woman, Lilian Baylis. Miss Baylis (1874–1937) was running the Old Vic Theatre at Waterloo, in south London, presenting a repertory of classical plays at popular prices. Ninette de Valois joined forces with her, on the understanding that when Miss Baylis should eventually re-open the derelict Sadler's Wells Theatre in Islington, north London, to house an opera company, Ninette de Valois' ballet school and her dancers should form the nucleus of a permanent ballet company. This plan came to fruition in 1931, and the Vic-Wells ballet company and school, blessed with a permanent home, developed under de Valois' inspiring guidance. During the 1930s the solid foundations of a great national company – the Royal Ballet – were methodically laid. The school – a vital component in any enduring balletic venture – had a home; de Valois herself provided some important choreography, and early on took the vital decision to obtain authentic stagings of the great classics of 19th-century ballet. She invited Nicholas Sergueyev (1876–1951) to revive the repertory which he had supervised at the Maryinsky Theatre in St Petersburg before the Russian revolution and which he had preserved with notation, and by 1934, the infant Vic-Wells ballet was capable of staging *Giselle*, *Swan Lake*, *Coppélia* and *The Nutcracker*.

De Valois was also fortunate in being able to call upon a true classical ballerina to dance several of these great roles. This was Alicia Markova (b 1910) who had been engaged by Diaghilev in 1925 as a phenomenal child dancer, and who had thereafter become an increasingly important member of the Ballet Russe. Now she, and her partner Anton Dolin (b 1904), also British born and an ex-Diaghilev principal, were to lend their support to the fledgling company. (Markova had also appeared with the Rambert ballet in its early days.) In 1935 Markova left the Wells to form her own company with Anton Dolin; however de Valois had a young dancer on whom she pinned many of her hopes. This was Margot Fonteyn (b 1919) who was to take over several of Markova's roles. At the same

Right Isadora Duncan – a photograph taken in Munich in 1902. The simplicity and innocence of Isadora's pose are typical of her at the very beginning of her European fame. Of actual technique she may have had very little – her dancing was often inspired by the moment – but Isadora had genius. She was a great liberator, both of men's ideas about dancing and about dancing itself, and we are all still in her debt.
Far Right Lynn Seymour in Ashton's *Five Brahms Waltzes in the Manner of Isadora Duncan.* When he was a young man Sir Frederick Ashton saw Isadora Duncan dance, and his phenomenal memory, sharp eye and understanding of dance mean that these waltzes (created in 1976) convey something of Isadora's quality, particularly since they were made for Lynn Seymour.
Below Antoinette Sibley as Titania in Ashton's *The Dream* with the Royal Ballet. In 1964, the Royal Ballet staged a programme of three ballets inspired by Shakespeare's writings. Sir Frederick Ashton turned to Mendelssohn's incidental music to *A Midsummer Night's Dream* and created a work of real mid-summer magic in which the story of the four lovers lost in a wood was combined with the quarrels between Titania and Oberon.
Below right Monica Mason as the Black Queen in Ninette de Valois' *Checkmate* for the Royal Ballet. Its theme is of a game of chess played between Love and Death, with Death triumphant through the treachery of his agent, the Black Queen. The role of the Black Queen has given fine opportunities to many ballerinas: outstanding nowadays is Monica Mason.

52

Above Antoinette Sibley and Anthony Dowell in the final scene of Ashton's *Cinderella* for the Royal Ballet. *Cinderella* is a great land-mark in British ballet. It was Ashton's first full-length work, and in it he carried on the tradition of big classic ballets which had been part of the foundation of the Royal Ballet. Prokofiev's beautiful score had been written for the Leningrad State Kirov Ballet; Ashton used it to make an English classic, combining elements from traditional pantomime (he and Sir Robert Helpmann were enormously funny as the Ugly Sisters) with the 19th century formula of a spectacular ballet based on a familiar fairy tale.

Right Lynn Seymour and Anthony Dowell in *A Month in the Country* with the Royal Ballet. Created in 1976 by Sir Frederick Ashton, and his first major work for some years, this ballet is based on Turgenyev's play *A Month in the Country*, and studies the nature of love, and more specifically the effect that a handsome young tutor has on a Russian provincial household in the middle of the last century. The leading roles were given to Lynn Seymour, as Natalya Petrovna, the mistress of the household, and Anthony Dowell as Belyayev, the tutor. Their performances, like those of the entire Royal Ballet cast, were superlative. Seymour and Dowell are shown

at the very end of the ballet, when the young tutor, whose romantic image has played such havoc with the emotions of both Natalya and of her young ward, is about to leave. Unseen by the unhappy Natalya Petrovna, he kisses the ribbons of her dress, and hurries away.

Below The Royal Ballet with Margot Fonteyn and Rudolf Nureyev in the ballroom scene from Kenneth MacMillan's *Romeo and Juliet*. This scene shows the Capulet ball, a few moments before Romeo catches sight of Juliet for the first time, and the tragedy gets under way. Romeo, on the left, is still flirting with Rosaline, and Juliet, at the foot of

the steps, is shyly greeting Paris (Derek Rencher) to whom she has just become betrothed. In the centre are Lord and Lady Capulet (Michael Somes and Julia Farron), and at the extreme right is Tybalt (David Drew). The designs are by Nicholas Georgiadis, a very distinguished stage decorator and artist who has worked with MacMillan on several of his major works. The opulence of renaissance dress is magnificently captured, and the excellence of Nicholas Georgiadis' designs lies not only in their visual splendour but also in the fact that the setting is speedily adaptable for use in the thirteen scenes which make up the ballet.

time de Valois had an exceptionally gifted dramatic dancer in Robert Helpmann (b1909) who had already partnered Markova, and who was to become the company's leading male star. Two other great formative talents were also to contribute to the health of this national company. Constant Lambert (1905–1951) was a composer and conductor of magnificent gifts – he had written a score for Diaghilev when only 20 – which he dedicated to the service of ballet for most of his life. He arranged scores, composed, conducted, and – very importantly – acted as artistic guide and counsellor to the company.

In 1935 Frederick Ashton, whose talents as a choreographer had been discovered by Marie Rambert, came to join the enterprise at Sadler's Wells Theatre. He had already created ballets for the company, but now his permanent association led to the composition of a series of major works – many starring Margot Fonteyn – which helped to create a style of classical dancing for the company. By 1939, the Sadler's Wells Ballet (as the company was now called) was firmly rooted, and could undertake its most important staging – a revival of *The Sleeping Beauty* with Fonteyn and Helpmann in the leading roles.

With the outbreak of war the company undertook extensive touring which took it throughout the British Isles. In the process the company acquired a new and faithful audience who were to ensure its popularity in time of peace. During these war years, the contribution of Robert Helpmann as choreographer (with ballets like *Hamlet* and *Miracle in the Gorbals*) and principal dancer was vitally important. With peace came the great opportunity. In 1946 the Royal Opera House, Covent Garden was re-opened as a theatre (after war-time service as a dance-hall) and de Valois was asked to transfer her company there. On 21 February 1946, with an opulent new version of *The Sleeping Beauty*, Fonteyn and Helpmann in the leading roles and Constant Lambert conducting, the Sadler's Wells Ballet entered a new phase in its history. But the Sadler's Wells Theatre was not abandoned. Dame Ninette formed a second company there – the Sadler's Wells Theatre Ballet. Under the guidance of Ursula Moreton and Peggy van Praagh it was to become a cradle for much of the new young talent of the post-war years. This was an exciting time for British ballet: the Sadler's Wells Ballet flourished at Covent Garden, with Frederick Ashton creating a stream of important ballets, many of them designed around the talents of Margot Fonteyn, who was hailed as a great ballerina; the second company at Sadler's Wells Theatre was encouraging new young dancers and most important, a second generation of choreographers (notably John Cranko, and within a few years, Kenneth MacMillan). Within three years the Sadler's Wells Ballet was to be known as a company of international stature following its first appearance in North America: audiences in New York and throughout America and Canada acclaimed not only Margot Fonteyn and Helpmann, but a whole string of outstanding dancers. The world was now to become aware of the English style of dancing and choreography, and of the importance of the classic repertory which was so carefully preserved and presented by what was acknowledged as the British national company.

Ballet was enormously popular. Britain received visits from many important foreign companies, notably New York City Ballet in 1950 and Ballet Theatre from America in 1946; and by the daring young French company – Les Ballets des Champs Elysées (also in 1946) – led by Roland Petit, who continued the Diaghilev tradition of employing outstanding artists to decorate his work. The Ballets Russes, alas, now seemed dead in Europe: de Basil returned in 1947 to give audiences a last glimpse of pre-war magic, but the standard of presentation was disappointing, and the company soon disbanded. Much more exciting was the arrival in London in 1956 of the real Russian ballet, the Bolshoy Ballet from Moscow, with the incomparable Ulanova as its star. The grandeur of the Russians' dancing was to thrill Britain, and thereafter the visits of the Bolshoy Ballet and the aristocratic Kirov from Leningrad (the former Maryinsky Theatre troupe) were to set standards of technical excellence which inspired dancers and public alike. The final establishment of the Sadler's Wells Ballet came in 1956 when Dame Ninette's endeavours were crowned with the granting of a Royal Charter: the Sadler's Wells Ballet and School (which had also flourished wonderfully since the war) were now to become the Royal Ballet. During the next decade, it could be seen how the influence and example of Dame Ninette's work was extending world-wide. Celia Franca (b 1921), a former dancer with both Rambert and the Sadler's Wells Ballets, went to Canada and laboured magnificently to bring about the creation of the National Ballet of Canada. Peggy van Praagh (b 1910), also a former graduate of the Rambert and Sadler's Wells organizations, went to Australia in 1961 to found the Australian Ballet. In 1961 John Cranko (1927–1973) went to Stuttgart from London to revitalize the Stuttgart Ballet and within a dozen years had made it an internationally acclaimed company. Cranko was a member of that generation of common-wealth dancers who hurried to London at the war's end to study at the Sadler's Wells School and then progress into the company (among his contemporaries were Nadia Nerina, Maryon Lane, Alexander Grant, Elaine Fifield, David Poole and Rowena Jackson, all of whom were to be vitally important as members of the Royal Ballet).

In 1964 Dame Ninette de Valois retired as director of the company she had founded, to be succeeded by Sir Frederick Ashton. Ashton's choreography had become the hallmark of the British national style, and it was particularly important that although he still continued to produce important short ballets, he also embarked upon a series of full-length works which were the logical continuation of the classical traditions he had inherited from Marius Petipa. In 1948 his three-act *Cinderella* was staged at the Royal Opera House. Thereafter, he created *Sylvia* (1952), *Ondine* (1958), *La Fille mal Gardée* (1960) and *The Two Pigeons* (1961) as full-length ballets for the Royal Ballet, and a *Romeo and Juliet* (1955) for the Royal Danish Ballet.

This tradition of full-length works has been continued by the man who succeeded Ashton in 1970 as director of the Royal Ballet, Kenneth MacMillan. MacMillan (b 1929) was another product of the Royal Ballet, moving from school to company, who started to create ballets in 1955. His first full-length work, *Romeo and Juliet*, was staged in 1965, and after three years leave of absence when he went to Berlin to direct the Deutsche Oper Ballet, he returned as Director of the Royal Ballet in 1970. For that company he has created many short works, and has continued the Ashton tradition by producing two further full-length works – *Anastasia* (1971) and *Manon* (1974).

Above Michael Coleman in *Elite Syncopations* with the Royal Ballet. In 1974 Kenneth MacMillan used the music of Scott Joplin for a rag-time romp for his company. Since then *Elite Syncopations* has become enormously popular. Its costumes, by Ian Spurling, are among the wittiest we know, and Michael Coleman gives a buoyant and amusing performance in the solo created for him.

Top right Lesley Collier in *Elite Syncopations* with the Royal Ballet. One of the Royal Ballet's leading young ballerinas, Lesley Collier is seen here in a comic solo variation, a burlesque of a stick and top-hat routine. Lesley Collier combines a sparkling classical technique with a sure dramatic gift and her roles range from Lise in *La Fille mal Gardée* to Juliet and Odette/Odile.

Top Far right Lynn Seymour and David Wall in Glen Tetley's *Voluntaries* with the Royal Ballet. Created as a memorial to John Cranko, *Voluntaries* uses the Poulenc organ concerto and is one of Tetley's most 'classical' ballets.

Right Marion Tait in Jack Carter's *Shukumei* for the Sadler's Wells Royal Ballet. Jack Carter retold a Japanese tale in *Shukumei* which he created for the Royal Ballet's touring company in 1975. Marion Tait, a very gifted young dancer, took the leading role of a bride who avenges her husband's murder by killing his three assassins.

Far right Wayne Eagling in *The Four Seasons* with the Royal Ballet. Wayne Eagling is one of the Royal Ballet's most exceptional artists: a virtuoso dancer who is also a sensitive dramatic performer. In *The Four Seasons* (1975) Kenneth MacMillan choreographed a balletic show-piece to display the sheer brilliance of his company, and in the 'Spring' section he made fine use of the extraordinary speed and fluency of Wayne Eagling's style.

Left Merle Park and Anthony Dowell in *Shadowplay*. Antony Tudor has spent many years in America, but in 1967 he returned to his native London to create his first ballet for The Royal Ballet at Covent Garden. This was *Shadowplay*, which starred Anthony Dowell as a young man awakening to the problems of growing up and understanding himself. Merle Park was the outstanding interpreter of the 'Celestial', a being whom the young man has to battle with. Merle Park, Rhodesian born, is one of the many exceptionally gifted Commonwealth artists who have brought so much to the Royal Ballet.

Below Anthony Dowell and Antoinette Sibley in Kenneth MacMillan's *Manon* with the Royal Ballet. In 1974 Kenneth MacMillan created his third full-length ballet at the Royal Opera House. MacMillan is one of the few choreographers in the world able to produce long narrative ballets using the resources of a large classical company. The story is adapted from an 18th century French novel, which tells how a young girl, Manon Lescaut, is corrupted by the vicious society of Paris; how the young Chevalier des Grieux falls in love with her; and how Manon is tragically deported to the swamps of Louisiana. Antoinette Sibley and Anthony Dowell as Manon and des Grieux are seen in one of the moving pas de deux which lie at the heart of the ballet.

Right Lynn Seymour in the first act of *Anastasia*. Lynn Seymour is the most gifted dramatic ballerina of her generation. Sometimes there occurs an extraordinary, creative relationship between a choreographer and a ballerina; she inspires his ballets; he is, in turn, eager to develop her powers even further through new and demanding roles. The Royal Ballet has been exceptionally fortunate, first, in the association between Sir Frederick Ashton and Dame Margot Fonteyn, which lasted for 30 years, and secondly in the rewarding union of talents between Kenneth MacMillan and Lynn Seymour. In the early days of both their careers, MacMillan created several important dramatic and lyric roles which revealed Lynn Seymour's importance as a dancer, and in 1966, when they both went to work in Berlin for three years, MacMillan choreographed a one-act *Anastasia* for her. This dealt with the mysterious figure of Mme Anna Anderson who claimed to be the Grand Duchess Anastasia, sole survivor of the Bolshevik assassination of the Russian Imperial Family in 1918. When MacMillan returned to The Royal Ballet as its director he expanded his idea of *Anastasia* into a three-act ballet. Its first two acts show the world of the Russian Imperial family, the last act deals with Mme Anderson's suffering as she tried to establish her identity. The ballet was a magnificent work, and Lynn Seymour is seen here in Act I, as the 14-year-old Grand Duchess Anastasia. Her entrance in the ballet is probably unique: she appears on roller-skates, an historical fact since there are films which show the real Grand Duchess enjoying this sport.

Below Barry McGrath in *Pineapple Poll* as staged by the Sadler's Wells Royal Ballet. John Cranko created this, one of his happiest comic ballets, in 1951. It was inspired by Gilbert and Sullivan: Gilbert's Bab Ballads provided the story of the irresistible Captain Belaye who charms all the girls of Portsmouth harbour, and Sullivan's music was arranged for the score. Illustrated is a moment in scene 1 when the Captain is being manhandled by his crew who are far from amused at the way their girl friends are attracted by the dashing Captain.

While the Royal Ballet at Covent Garden was established as a national institution, its second company – now known as the Sadler's Wells Royal Ballet following its return to a home base at Sadler's Wells Theatre in 1976 – undertook a considerable touring schedule in the regions. As part of the ballet boom during and after the war, several other classical companies were launched. International Ballet led by Mona Inglesby toured classical stagings and a small modern repertory from its inception in 1941 until it was disbanded in 1953. In 1948 Alicia Markova and Anton Dolin returned to London after ten years spent working in America where they had been hailed to be among the greatest ballet stars. So great was their success that in 1949 they embarked upon a regional tour which led to the founding in the following year of London Festival Ballet (named after the Festival of Britain). The company offered classic stagings, revivals of the Diaghilev repertory, and new works, and provided audiences with a wonderful opportunity to see some of the greatest international stars as guest artists. Under the administration of Dr Julian Braunsweg the company flourished despite the absence of any government subsidy – it is worth recording that ballet, like the other performing arts, had now become so prohibitively expensive that official financial support was needed, even with continually full houses. Festival Ballet toured all round Britain and then embarked upon lengthy and very successful world tours; the acquisition of subsidies from the Greater London Council and the Arts Council were well merited. After some managerial changes, a new artistic director was appointed: Beryl Grey, formerly a ballerina with the Royal Ballet, took charge of the company in 1968, and has directed it since then with Paul Findlay as administrator. The company policy of classic staging and Diaghilev repertory as a basis for its work has remained stable, and over the years a varied collection of more contemporary ballets has also been presented.

Ballet Rambert, the oldest of British companies, had long suffered from the fact that the choreographers and dancers who had been discovered and encouraged by Marie Rambert, often left for greater opportunities with larger companies: Frederick Ashton made over a dozen elegant works for Ballet Rambert during the early 1930s – such small gems as *Les Masques* and *Foyer de Danse* featured Alicia Markova; his early comedy *Façade* was preserved by Rambert after it was created for the Camargo Society (which presented brief seasons of ballet in London after Diaghilev's death). Antony Tudor created two of his greatest ballets – *Dark Elegies* and *Jardin aux Lilas* – in the mid 1930s; Andrée Howard (1908–1968) made her amazing *Lady into Fox* in 1939, and two years later created a delicate masterpiece, *La Fête Etrange*; while Walter Gore (b 1910) and Frank Staff (1918–1971) continued the amazing creative record of the Rambert company into the 1940s and 1950s.

But important choreographers such as these had to move on to the challenges of bigger companies. Ashton joined the Sadler's Wells Ballet; Tudor and Andrée Howard both went to America; Walter Gore formed his own company and worked throughout Europe and in Australia; Frank Staff went to South Africa. Dancers, too, naturally wanted more experience, and John Gilpin, a Rambert graduate and one of the brightest young dancers Britain had produced, made a stellar career as the principal male dancer of London Festival Ballet. Despite the loss of fine artists since her earliest seasons Rambert continued to find further talent, and the list of Rambert dancers and choreographers is one of outstanding talent and achievement. After the war a tour of Australia was tremendously successful, although by the end the company had lost much of its personnel. In the following years the need to tour in competition with larger companies was to lead to near disintegration. Nevertheless, excellent stagings (including a fine *Giselle* and *La Sylphide*) were still preserved, and a talented new choreographer, Norman Morrice, was discovered. It was Morrice, who, with Dame Marie, revitalized the company in 1966 with a total change of policy. Inspired by the example of the Nederlands Dans Theater (a ballet company dedicated to adventurous work which combined classic and Modern Dance) Ballet Rambert was re-formed as a small troupe of soloists and its repertory was re-forged: the influence of Glen Tetley (an American choreographer) was important in showing a way in which classic and modern could be combined. Once again – as in the 1930s – Ballet Rambert was doing pioneer work and was in the forefront of the growing interest in Modern Dance. In addition to the ballets of Glen Tetley, new works by Norman Morrice provided the mainstay of the repertory. Within a short while several other choreographers had emerged from within the ranks of the company – a typical facet of the Rambert system. Notable among these is Christopher Bruce, one of the outstanding dancers of our time, and John Chesworth, now director (with Bruce) of the company. The Rambert tradition of encouraging creativity among its dancers is still maintained today in its work-shop seasons co-presented with the Central School of Art and Design.

One of the great champions of Modern Dance in Britain is Robin Howard, a philanthropist who had been inspired by the work of Martha Graham and through his financial generosity, had made possible her visits to Britain. At first British audiences did not appreciate Modern Dance, but persistence paid off: the visits of Graham, of Merce Cunningham, Paul Taylor, Jose Limón and Alvin Ailey with their companies began to attract an appreciative audience. Howard's next move was to plan the establishment of a

Left Dancers of the London Contemporary Dance Theatre in Robert Cohan's *Waterless Method of Swimming Instruction*. As the title implies, this ballet by Robert Cohan makes use of many of the movements of swimming and diving. While much of it is athletically exciting, there are also moments of humour – and the all-white decor and costumes by Ian Murray Clarke suggest that the ballet is taking place in the emptied swimming pool on the deck of an ocean liner.

Right Christopher Bruce in Glen Tetley's *Pierrot Lunaire* with Ballet Rambert. *Pierrot Lunaire* is one of the most accomplished first works by a choreographer of recent times. Glen Tetley created it in New York in 1962, and in 1967 he revived it for Ballet Rambert. It is a small masterpiece in which the traditional figures of Pierrot, Columbine and Brighella play out the basic conflict between innocence and experience. With only three characters the ballet yet manages to say a great deal about human nature, and it gains enormously in the Rambert staging from the presence of Christopher Bruce as Pierrot.

Bruce, one of the greatest dancers in Britain, is also a choreographer of rare qualities.

Top right Dancers of London Contemporary Dance Theatre in Robert Cohan's *Nymphéas*. *Nymphéas* are waterlilies, and there is a great series of paintings under this title in which the French Impressionist master Claude Monet caught on canvas the constantly changing play of light on water. Robert Cohan was inspired by this same idea to choreograph a ballet to Debussy music which evoked some of these luminous effects in dance.

Above Dancers of Ballet Rambert in Norman Morrice's *That is the Show*. In 1971 Norman Morrice, one of the most distinguished choreographers of Ballet Rambert used Luciano Berio's *Sinfonia* for a plotless ballet of great beauty. It took some of its inspiration from the spoken text that is part of the score – intriguing snatches of çonversation and commentary – but like many modern works it leaves the audience free to make up its own mind about the ballet's subject.

British dance company and school based upon the Graham technique. To this end he invited Martha Graham's support, and she sent several of her dancers to work with students in London – notably Robert Cohan (b 1925). From this small beginning there developed rapidly the school and company now known as the London Contemporary Dance Theatre. Premises were found in a former army drill hall which was converted into a theatre and teaching studio. This is The Place, the present home of London Contemporary Dance Theatre. Under the guidance of Robert Cohan as artistic director and chief choreographer, the company has established itself in less than a decade as the finest Modern Dance company in Europe. Cohan had 'naturalised' Graham's style to create an authentically British method of Modern Dance: his artists were encouraged to create work, and there now exists a most healthy and exciting nucleus of choreographers who provide the repertory of the London Contemporary Dance Theatre. Among these we must note particularly Siobhan Davies, Robert North, and Micha Bergese. Robert Cohan is an inspiring creator and teacher, and in recent years the company has embarked upon an important programme of working within colleges and schools throughout Britain to encourage a greater interest and participation in dance at every level.

While London has inevitably remained the centre of dance activity, there have been some successful attempts to establish dance in the regions. Most important of these has been the creation of The Scottish Ballet. In 1957 Elizabeth West (1927–1962) and Peter Darrell (b 1929) founded a small company in Bristol. Western Theatre Ballet was dedicated to the presentation of new ballets whose interest was both in their dramatic content and in their use of contemporary themes. Darrell's choreography was well suited to this ideal, and after several years of courageous touring under the most difficult financial circumstances, Western Theatre Ballet was recognized as a vital part of the British dance scene. In 1969, with Arts Council support, the company was transferred to Glasgow to become the Scottish Ballet, where it has now established itself firmly. Both classics and modern repertory are now offered, and its tours in the Northern part of the British Isles, as well as internationally, have made it a cultural force of some renown.

Below Dancers of the Scottish ballet in *Tales of Hoffmann* by Peter Darrell. As director of the Scottish Ballet, Peter Darrell has created four full length ballets: *Hoffmann* is a clever adaptation of Offenbach's operetta for the dance stage.

Below right Mikhail Barishnikov and Marianna Tcherkassky with dancers of American Ballet Theatre in Twyla Tharp's *Push Comes to Shove*. Twyla Tharp, an extremely gifted young American choreographer, created this exciting new work in 1975 for these dancers. It is a ballet combining wit and beautiful dancing; using both rag-time music and a classical symphony (No. 82 by Haydn) for its score. The dancers have tremendous fun throughout, not least with a bowler hat which passes from head to head. All Twyla Tharp's dance-works, whether for her own company or for 'ballet' companies, demand the most meticulous timing and precision, although the resulting choreography can often look easy and spontaneous. Anyone fortunate enough to have seen her dances, either in the flesh or on TV will remember their characteristic elegance. For Mikhail Barishnikov *Push Comes to Shove* provides diabolically difficult and exciting dances, which he performs with tremendous zest.

Following page Dancers of Martha Graham's Company in *Seraphic Dialogue*. Martha Graham's dance-work about St Joan, instead of telling the story as straight narrative, concentrates upon three sides of Joan's personality: the maid, the warrior, and the martyr, represented by the three seated dancers. Joan herself is kneeling in *arabesque* in front of them. Behind can be seen the saints whose voices have directed her destiny and who are waiting to receive her into glory. An important feature of all Graham's work is the stage design, which has always been integral to the dance action rather than mere scene setting. A favoured designer for many years has been the Japanese-American Isamu Noguchi, one of the greatest of all contemporary stage designers. The beautiful simplicity of his work is typified by the golden structures which are used in *Seraphic Dialogue*.

Page 65 top Dancers of the Alwin Nikolais company in *Tensile Involvement*. Alwin Nikolais has devised a special form of dance which uses light and stage properties quite as much as choreographed movement to achieve amazing and magical effects. In

AMERICA

The United States of America is unique in having had a fully developed dance style before the classic ballet had really put down firm roots throughout the continent. As already mentioned, the example of Isadora Duncan had inspired Ruth St Denis and her husband Ted Shawn; in turn they provided the incentive for the most influential figure in American Modern Dance – Martha Graham. After working with the Denishawn School and company. Graham left to work on her own, and thus started Modern Dance's pattern of an amoeba-like separation from the main cell: dancers work with one company or teacher, then leave to form their own groups, and from this group in turn other dancers split away, and so continue the growth and development of new dance units. Both technique and ideas about what Modern Dance can express are thus constantly renewed. Despite continuing financial problems, which often bring about the demise of these small dance groups, the richness of the dance activity in the United States is very impressive.

But it is to Martha Graham that we have to look first, since it was she who provided the foundations that have existed for over half a century – a technique of training which is as carefully worked-out as that of classic ballet. From her first performances in 1926, through the arduous years when she was building up a repertory as well as training dancers, Graham has been one of the greatest innovators in the history of dance. Her technique evolved as she made ballets. She rejected the conscious beauty and the upward movement of classic ballet in favour of a style that made use of the simple act of breathing in and out which resulted in the basic rhythm of 'contraction and release'. She sought to show the importance of effort in dance rather than classic ballet's desire to conceal it. She accepted the existence of gravity as a force to use and to react against. Her early style was often angular rather than elongated; costuming was severe in shape while allowing the dancers total freedom of movement (Graham costumes are always a vital part in the dance). Over the years Graham has made dances that deal with the pioneering American spirit (*Appalachian Spring* and *Frontier*) as well as themes taken from classical drama and religion (*Clytemnestra*, *Seraphic Dialogue*).

Now in her eighties, Graham can see that the style of dancing which she has developed has been universally accepted as a vital artistic force. Among her contemporaries, Doris Humphrey was also important, as was also Humphrey's pupil and associate, Jose Limón (1908–1972). It is from certain Graham associates, like Merce Cunningham (b 1919) and Paul Taylor (b 1930) that some of the most exciting new ideas in Modern Dance have come. Having absorbed Graham's teaching, Cunningham was in his turn prepared to break all the rules and to adopt natural activities like sport, even bicycle riding, as material for dances. Over the years his dances have become almost 'classical' in their concern with movement pure and simple – narrative and drama have been left behind, and the eye is delighted simply by the qualities of the dancers' movements. Cunningham is happy to let elements of chance enter into his dances, notably in some of the scores he uses by the very adventurous composer John Cage, and also in the order in which certain dances will be performed or have even been composed. Paul Taylor, who worked with Cunningham, has also extended the boundaries of dancing. Some of his works are lyrically beautiful (like *Aureole*, which is danced by the Royal Danish Ballet); others are melodramatic (*Big Bertha*), and his two-act *Orbs* is one of the dance masterpieces of our time. Additionally, Taylor has a wonderful sense of humour, and pieces like *Book of Beasts* or *Public Domain* are hilariously funny.

From Taylor's company came another immensely exciting creator: Twyla Tharp. Her early works belonged to a time (the 1960s) when Modern Dance was very concerned with experiments about where to dance, how to dance and what could be included in dance. (In one of her early works she broke raw eggs on to the stage.) During the past six years she has evolved a style of the greatest brilliance and discipline, and her company is composed of exceptional virtuoso dancers for whom she has made a series of dazzling pieces of the most intricate difficulty and precision. *Eight Jelly Rolls, The Bix Pieces* – recent triumphs – were inspired by Twyla Tharp's fascination with the popular music and dances of America, and in 1973 she staged a tremendously successful piece *Deuce Coupe* (with music by The Beach Boys) for the Joffrey Ballet. In 1975, she composed a masterly work using the talents of a classical company – American Ballet Theatre – and one of the finest classical dancers of our time: Mikhail Barishnikov. This was *Push comes to Shove* which

contrast to most other dance companies, who emphasise the human form, Nikolais's dancers are often transformed into un-human or other-worldly shapes. The illustration shows a more conventional use of the dancers, but their manipulation of elastic cords creates a new kind of spacial geometry through which they move. The electronic scores for the dances are also composed by Nikolais, who

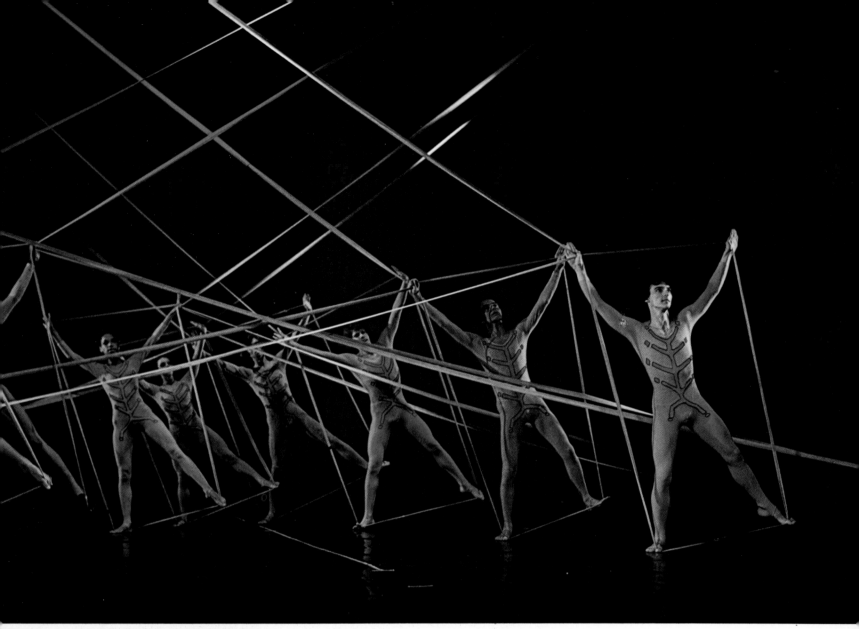

combined a Haydn symphony and piano rags, and was hailed as one of the most exciting new works of the year.

Two other rather different companies must be mentioned here: those of Alvin Ailey and Alwin Nikolais. Alvin Ailey (b 1931) was first recognized as one of the most exciting Black dancers in America. In 1957 he decided to form a company that would express the many facets of Black American dance, from jazz and tap dancing, through Modern Dance to the rhythms of ethnic dancing in the Caribbean and in Africa. His own choreography has been admired – notably *Revelations* which takes Negro spirituals for its theme – and his company has achieved world-wide success on its many tours. Very different is the work of Alwin Nikolais (b 1912), a magician of light and movement. Nikolais is most concerned with visual effects obtained through the complex and exciting manipulation of light and fabric. His dancers become completely transformed into odd, beautiful and mysterious shapes, and Nikolais' skill in devising both lighting and sound accompaniment, as well as choreography, has been vitally important in revealing new possibilities in theatrical presentation.

We have mentioned but a few of the multitudinous Modern dance troupes who appear throughout the United States: many of these groups find financial support and enthusiastic audiences in the colleges which feature dance in their education programmes the length and breadth of America. The importance of this contribution by colleges to dance is very great: in the 1930s Martha Graham found a haven at Bennington College in Vermont, and this tradition of college involvement in dance is one of the reasons for the vitality of the American dance scene.

Parallel with the expansion of Modern Dance has been the development of classic ballet in America. The most important figure is, of course, George Balanchine, whose New York City Ballet is one of the great classical ensembles in the world. Balanchine's presence in the USA is due initially to the idealism of Lincoln Kirstein (b 1907), a poet, author and philanthropist of the arts, who was determined that the classical ballet should put down roots in America. He had been a great admirer of Balanchine's work for Diaghilev, and in 1933, he, together with Edward M. M. Warburg, provided the enthusiasm and the funds which would bring Balanchine to America. There Balanchine was to start a

is thus able to create a totally unified work.
Above Dancers of the Alvin Ailey company in *Revelations*. Of all the ballets presented by Alvin Ailey's company, one in particular seems to sum up everything that is best in this very popular troupe: Ailey's own *Revelations*. Inspired by the Negro Spirituals, *Revelations* expresses the hope, terror, melancholy and joy found in these beautiful songs.

Right Violin Concerto was choreographed by George Balanchine to the Stravinsky concerto, and was first given during the New York City Ballet's Stravinsky Festival in 1972. It is a perfect example of Balanchine's plotless realizations of music. For nearly fifty years, dating from the *Apollo* for Diaghilev in 1928, Balanchine and Stravinsky combined their talents to enrich ballet in the 20th century. The two men were great friends, and Stravinsky felt that in Balanchine he had found the perfect choreographic interpreter of his music. For his part Balanchine wrote: 'Stravinsky's music altogether satisfies me. It makes me comfortable. When I listen to a score by him I am moved – I don't like the word inspired – to try to make visible not only the rhythm, melody and harmony, but even the timbres of the instruments. For if I could write music it seems to me that this is how I would want it to sound.' *Violin Concerto* is the latest in a long line of masterly ballets that Balanchine has conceived: they are among the chief masterpieces of dance in our time. In the centre of our picture is one of the City Ballet's leading dancers: Kay Mazzo. The simplicity of costuming and staging, just practice clothes, is typical of the design for many Balanchine works.

Below right Suzanne Farrell and Peter Martins in Balanchine's *Chaconne* for New York City Ballet. George Balanchine has used the music of Gluck's *Orpheus and Eurydice* on several occasions. He staged the opera in New York in 1936 – when the stuffy audiences at the Metropolitan Opera House were totally resistant to the importance of what Balanchine was doing – and in 1973 he made another version for the Paris Opéra. Most recently he has produced a suite of dances to the ballet music: under the title of *Chaconne* it has been hailed as a beautiful example of his ability to realize music in dance. Our illustration shows two of New York City Ballet's finest principals in his new version, first given in New York in 1976.

Right American Ballet Theatre dancers in *Fancy Free*. It is not often that a ballet inspires both a film and a stage musical but Jerome Robbins' first ballet for American Ballet Theatre, which he created in 1944, was successfully adapted for the screen and musical stage as *On The Town*. It is an extraordinary work in that it deals with every-day people. Three sailors on shore leave in New York visit a bar and try to pick up a girl each. This they don't achieve, but the fun they have in the process makes for one of the happiest ballets in any repertory in the world. It is a totally successful piece of Americana, and during the years since its creation it has never left the company repertory: succeeding generations of dancers have had wonderful fun as the sailors, who each in turn show off to the girls in brilliant dances in the bar. Robbins' career was launched by this ballet, and it is a tribute to his early brilliance that *Fancy Free* is still one of the greatest favourites with audiences wherever American Ballet Theatre plays it.

school and a company, with Kirstein always at his right hand to administer and support. Initially there were many problems: not least because America was just emerging from the financial crisis of the Depression, and was entering a phase of political isolation ·in which anything from Europe (even the arts) was viewed with some suspicion. By the late 1930s Balanchine had created a repertory for his American Ballet, but the war and financial problems were to force him to work on Broadway and in Hollywood for some years. It was in 1946 that Balanchine and Kirstein formed the Ballet Society in New York for seasons of dance performances; from this there came the invitation in 1948 to establish the company at the New York City Center, and in October 1948 the New York City Ballet – as such – came into existence. From then on the company's success was rapid: Balanchine had brought his classic style from St Petersburg and had transformed it on the bodies of his athletic young American dancers to create an authentically American classic style; clean, swift and very much of the New World. He has composed a glorious series of ballets, many of them pure dance works, using scores that range from the concert repertory to George Gershwin, John Philip Sousa and electronic music. Balanchine also continued his artistic collaboration with Igor Stravinsky. This had begun with the staging of *Apollo* for the Diaghilev Ballet in 1928, and reached its culmination in the summer of 1972 when in homage to Stravinsky, who had died in the previous year, a festival of 31 ballets to Stravinsky scores was mounted by the City Ballet's choreographers. Chief among these associates of Balanchine is Jerome Robbins (b 1918). Robbins had first come to fame as a dancer with American Ballet Theatre, for whom he made his first, wildly successful ballet, *Fancy Free* in 1944. Robbins moved to New York City Ballet with whom he has been chiefly associated. He has also worked on Broadway – notably in staging *West Side Story* and producing such musicals as *Fiddler on the Roof*, and *The King and I*. For a time he directed his own company, Ballets USA, but the major part of his choreography in recent years has been presented by the New York City Ballet, and his recent *Dances at a Gathering* (1969) and *Goldberg Variations* (1971) have been recognized as masterly creations.

The other major classical company in America, American Ballet Theatre, gave its first performance under the direction of Lucia Chase (b 1907) and Richard Pleasant in January 1940. Over the years the company has presented a wide range of ballets and stars. Its policy has been based on the idea of presenting all kinds of ballet, from the Russian

classics and the Diaghilev repertory to contemporary American works. It has engaged some of the greatest choreographers and ballet stars of the past 30 years, and has given its vast public the opportunity to see works and dancers of world-wide importance. Unlike the New York City Ballet which avoids any sort of 'star-system', American Ballet Theatre welcomes stars: such exceptional artists as Erik Bruhn (b 1928), a flawless classical danseur from Copenhagen, Alicia Alonso (b 1917) the Cuban ballerina and today's brightest stars – Natalya Makarova and Mikhail Barishnikov – have found remarkable opportunities for work with the company. It also contains an impressive number of fine American dancers, notably Norah Kaye (b 1920) who during her career with the company was shown to be a great dramatic ballerina, particularly in the works staged for the company by Antony Tudor who had emigrated to America from London in 1939.

Classical ballet in the United States is not, of course, limited to these two companies. Across the continent there are many companies, indeed, the oldest American ballet company is that in San Francisco which was formed in 1933 by the émigré Russian dancer Adolf Bolm. In 1937 Willam Christensen became its director, and with his brother Lew guided its development, and today it maintains a healthy creativity under Lew Christensen and Michael Smuin. In Chicago the dancer and choreographer Ruth Page (b 1905) has fostered a great deal of ballet acivity in collaboration with the Chicago Opera, and other companies in Boston, Cincinnati, Philadelphia, Salt Lake City and other major cities continue valuable work.

In New York the choreographer Robert Joffrey (b 1930) has established a classical company which is now based at the New York City Center (vacant after Balanchine had transferred his company to the impressive theatrical complex at the Lincoln Center). The Joffrey Ballet repertory is a varied one, ranging from traditional works by Massine, Balanchine, Ashton, Bournonville, etc. to 'pop' works by Joffrey himself and his associate choreographer Gerald Arpino (b 1928) which include *Clowns*, *Astarte*, and *The Sacred Grove on Mount Tamalpais*.

One last company must be mentioned: the Dance Theatre of Harlem. In 1971 Arthur Mitchell (b 1934), a leading black dancer who had made a distinguished career with New York City Ballet, was impelled by the ideals of the Negro Civil Rights movement to pioneer a school of classical dance and subsequently a ballet company in Harlem, the predominantly negro quarter of New York. From the hundreds of young people who flocked to his classes, he selected and trained the ensemble known as the Dance Theatre of Harlem, which offers a part classic, part ethnic repertory of ballets and, besides regular New York seasons, has toured throughout America and overseas to great acclaim.

Above Jacques d'Amboise and Suzanne Farrell in *Apollo* with the New York City Ballet. *Apollo* is one of the most influential ballets of the 20th century. Choreographed by George Balanchine in 1928 to Stravinsky's noble score, the ballet tells of the birth of the god Apollo, and his meeting with three muses of poetry, mime and dance. Each in turn dances for him, seeking his approval, and it is Terpsichore, muse of Dance, whom he chooses as the best. At the ballet's end, he leads all three up to Mount Olympus. The importance of *Apollo* lies in the fact that in this work Balanchine discovered a way of reusing the classical dance style that revitalized it for 20th century ballet. Thereafter, Balanchine was recognized as the greatest choreographer of our time. The ballet is performed by many companies – but its best staging is, of course, by that of Balanchine's own company. Jacques d'Amboise is a fine Apollo, and he is seen here with Suzanne Farrell as Terpsichore in the pas de deux which lies at the heart of the ballet.

Above left Dumbarton Oaks Concerto was staged by Jerome Robbins for the New York City Ballet's Stravinsky Festival in 1972. Using Stravinsky's chamber concerto for string orchestra, Jerome Robbins made a ballet in the setting of a tennis party. The dancers look as if they might have strayed in from a musical comedy of the 1920s; their dances, though, were composed with all Robbins' usual skilled craftsmanship. The central couple in our picture are Allegra Kent and Anthony Blum.

RUSSIA

The Revolution of 1917 affected every aspect of life in Russia, and the ballet, like all the arts, was subjected to revolutionary fervour. Because the ballet was so associated with the Tsar's court and the aristocracy, it may be thought surprising that it survived at all, but the new Commissar for Public Education, Anatoly Lunacharsky, was both a friend of Lenin and a devotee and critic of the ballet. He pointed out that there was no reason why the people should not inherit the glories of the ballet as they were inheriting everything else in Russia. So, after some difficult years, the ballet flourished once more, and the audiences who came to admire the great classics of the 19th century were now drawn from factories rather than palaces. It is significant that the central government moved to Moscow from Petersburg, and the Bolshoy Ballet in Moscow was gradually regarded as the showcase for the new socialist theories of ballet. The style of dancing and production in Moscow had, in any case, always been different, more colourfully dramatic than in aristocratic Petersburg. In Moscow, at the beginning of this century this had been developed by Alexander Gorsky (1871–1924). Gorsky re-staged many of Petipa's ballets at the Bolshoy and made them more obviously dramatic. His own ballets also had considerable theatrical vitality, and even today there is still a distinction to be made between the Moscow and Leningrad (as Petersburg was renamed) styles of dancing. After the Revolution, although many of the old ballets were preserved, new full-length works were gradually produced which expressed the themes of a socialist society: instead of enchanted princesses and fairy tales, ordinary people now became the heroes of ballet. In the first true Soviet ballet, *The Red Poppy*, staged in 1927, the plot showed Russian sailors helping Chinese peasants in an uprising. Later works turned to other revolutionary themes (*The Flames of Paris* which dealt with the French Revolution of 1789), or to Russian and world literature: *Romeo and Juliet, Fountain of Bakhchisaray* (from a poem by Pushkin) and most recently Tolstoy's *Anna Karenina*, or to history: *Spartacus*, the story of the Roman slaves' uprising, and *Ivan the Terrible*, about the Tsar who unified Russia in the 16th century.

But while the choreography may be accused of being too restricted in its themes and expression, the long tradition of great teaching in Russia has had a magnificent development thanks to the work of Agrippina Vaganova (1879–1951). Vaganova had been a

Below Mikhail Lavrovsky with members of the Bolshoy Ballet in *Spartacus*. Yury Grigorovich's spectacular treatment of the revolt of the slaves in Ancient Rome against the tyrant Crassus has become one of the best known Soviet Ballets since its creation in Moscow in 1968. Then, as now, the audiences are thrilled by the massed effects of legionaries and slaves, and by the dynamic dancing of all the Bolshoy company. In its quieter moments, which tell of the love of Spartacus for the slave girl Phrygia, Grigorovich created choreographic duets of touching emotional warmth. But it is the heroic dancing of the Bolshoy men which provides the main excitement of the work: they soar and surge over the stage with massive power – devouring space like astronauts. Mikhail Lavrovsky, one of the Bolshoy's outstanding artists, is shown here as Spartacus, surrounded by the rebel slaves: Lavrovsky's commanding pose tells everything about the vigour and dramatic force of his performance. The score by Aram Khachaturian contains music that is well known to people in Britain who have never seen the ballet: it is used to introduce BBC TV's *Onedin Line*.

ballerina at the Maryinsky Theatre in Petersburg, and after the Revolution she opened a school where she was to evolve a wonderful extension of the old classic style of dancing. Invited to become the chief teacher at the Leningrad State School, she trained dancers to use movements which were bigger and more space-consuming, with soaring leaps and more fluid and expressive arms and backs. The Vaganova pupils reflected something of the new exciting spirit of the age, but they retained the perfection of line and aristocracy of style that had always been the best quality of the old Petersburg dancers. So successful was Vaganova that her Leningrad teaching system was adopted throughout Russia, both in Moscow and in the many other theatres and schools which were established during the next decades. Today, thanks to her system, the magnificent qualities of Russian dancers are admired throughout the world. There still remains a certain difference between Leningrad dancers and those in the rest of the Soviet Union: artists like Natalya Makarova and Mikhail Barishnikov (two Leningrad stars who chose to work in the West) and the occasional visits of the Leningrad company (The Kirov State Theatre Ballet) remind us of the superlative distinction and nobility of the Vaganova style as it is maintained in Leningrad. Moscow dancers seem still more athletic and emotional: such great stars as Maya Plisetskaya, or Vladimir Vasiliev and his wife Ekaterina Maximova exemplify the Moscow style which is exultantly beautiful.

Ballet flourishes today throughout Russia probably more than anywhere else in the world, since it is a vastly popular entertainment for the entire nation, with thriving ballet companies in every major city of the Union of Socialist Republics. Although the Russian dancers excite universal admiration and awe, the same cannot always be said for the ballets that they dance. Because the arts in Russia are subject to some form of government control, the themes of ballets need to reflect the political ideals of the country, and are consequently often narrow in their range of subject. Modern plotless works, of the kind staged by Balanchine, are unknown; the idea that dance can be satisfying as pure dance without any need for a dramatic argument, or even a 'message' is foreign to Soviet ballet's ideals. Experiment of the kind that has brought Modern Dance to the fore in the West, and has so enlivened ballet throughout the rest of the world, is virtually unknown, and it is for this reason that certain dancers – Nureyev, Makarova and Barishnikov, for example – decided to leave Russia in search of new roles and more challenging choreography. These 'defectors' have had a profound influence on ballet dancers in the West. Even more so have been the visits of Soviet Ballet companies. In 1956 the Bolshoy Ballet from Moscow paid its first visit to Europe, performing at The Royal Opera House, Covent Garden. The effect of the Russian's big, free dance style, and the magic of their prima ballerina, Galina Ulanova, was a great inspiration. Ulanova (b 1910), Leningrad trained, was a supreme lyric artist, and her appearance in *Giselle* and *Romeo and Juliet* have been preserved on film for a grateful posterity.

FRANCE AND BELGIUM

Left Rimma Karelskaya in *Laurencia* with the Bolshoy Ballet. The story of *Laurencia* is a tragedy which tells of a peasants' revolt in Spain in the 15th century. The story is one naturally attractive to Soviet choreographers and audiences, and the celebrated Georgian dancer Vakhtang Chabukyany (for many years a star of the Leningrad ballet) made the ballet in 1939. It has always remained in the Soviet repertory since then, though nothing of it has been seen in the West, except a famous virtuoso pas de six. Here the Moscow ballerina Rimma Karelskaya is the heroine, Laurencia, in a superbly 'open' Bolshoy arabesque.

Below London Festival Ballet in Serge Lifar's *Noir et Blanc*. Among Serge Lifar's best known ballets is the grand display-piece *Noir et Blanc* that he created in 1943 for the ballet company, the Paris Opéra. The ballet is danced to part of the fine score that Edouard Lalo wrote for his two-act *Namouna* which had been staged at the Opéra in 1882. Lifar's choreography for *Noir et Blanc* is both demanding and effective. The ballet is still presented by the Paris Opéra, and also by London Festival Ballet, who are seen here in its final tableau.

During the latter part of the 19th century the performance and appreciation of ballet in France, as elsewhere in Western Europe, had declined enormously. Nevertheless, Paris still remained the artistic centre of Europe, and Paris's acclaim meant success: it was to that city that Diaghilev brought his Ballet Russe. Although the Opéra still maintained a ballet troupe, its work was not of great importance until 1930, when, following the death of Diaghilev, his last male star, Serge Lifar (b 1905), was invited to take over the ballet as director, choreographer and principal dancer. For the next three decades, until his retirement in 1958, Lifar brought the Opéra back into the limelight, creating a large number of ballets, and working with a series of superlative ballerinas. Foremost among these were Olga Spessivtseva (b 1895), arguably the greatest ballerina of our century, who was initially a star in Petersburg and later worked with Diaghilev, Yvette Chauviré (b 1917) a superb French ballerina, and the Franco-Russian star Nina Vyroubova (b 1921). During the Lifar years the Opéra School, the home of great dance tradition, produced a series of exceptional male and female artists, and today it continues to feed the Opéra company with outstanding performers. But with Lifar's departure in 1958 the Opéra fell upon confused times, and since then it has seemed to lack any very positive artistic policy. In spite of this its repertory is continually enlarged with the work of guest choreographers who have ranged from Yury Grigorovich (b 1927), director of the Bolshoy Ballet in Moscow, to Merce Cunningham, Glen Tetley and Maurice Béjart (b 1927).

While the academic style was being preserved at the Opéra, more adventurous ideas were to be expressed at the war's end in 1944–45 when an extraordinary outburst of dance activity took place in Paris. This centred upon a young dancer trained at the Opéra, Roland Petit (b 1924). With the help of Boris Kochno, formerly secretary and assistant to Serge Diaghilev, and Irène Lidova, a French critic and writer he formed a new ballet company: Les Ballets des Champs Elysées. With the collaboration of many distinguished painters and musicians, with a group of young dancers, and with ballets choreographed by Petit, the Champs Elysées company astonished and delighted audiences by the beauty of its stagings, and the stylishness of its repertory. Its male star,

Jean Babilée (b 1923), was one of the most extraordinary dramatic and technical virtuosos of his time, and the company exemplified everything that Paris stood for in the arts: wit, elegance, and true *chic*. However, the Champs Elysées declined, lacking firm foundations. Roland Petit went on to form another company, the Ballets de Paris where he staged several exceptional ballets, particularly *Carmen* which he created for his wife Renée (Zizi) Jeanmaire (b 1924). During this time, several other interesting troupes were formed in France, and then fell on hard times, though not without making their artistic mark. One company in particular, the Grand Ballet du Marquis de Cuevas, did much to revive the glamour of the touring Ballet Russe, and it travelled the world with a fine collection of ballets and some outstandingly good dancers – Nina Vyroubova, Serge Golovine, Rosella Hightower, Georges Skibine, Marjorie Tallchief – until the death of the Marquis de Cuevas who had sustained the enterprise from his private funds. In passing it is worth noting that, to survive, the two prerequisites for a ballet company are a school and a resident choreographer; a permanent theatre can only be placed third on the list of requirements, together with a government subsidy (failing a patron with a bottomless pocket).

Left Michaël Denard and Ghislaine Thesmar in Jerome Robbins' *Afternoon of a Faun* at the Paris Opéra. Only a choreographer of great skill could dare to re-interpret a score so closely associated with the legendary Nijinsky. Jerome Robbins' version of Debussy's *L'Après-midi d'un Faune* is set in a ballet studio. A boy is resting languorously on the floor, and then starts to exercise. The ballet's quality is enhanced by the clever idea of making the proscenium opening seem the fourth, mirrored wall of the studio, so that the dancer, in looking at himself, is in fact looking directly at the audience without appearing to be aware of them. A young girl enters the studio to practice, and the couple's consciousness of each other is conveyed solely by their gaze into the mirror, without direct glances between them. They rehearse together still looking into the mirror, but finally the boy cannot resist giving the girl the gentlest of kisses on the cheek. The spell is broken, she leaves, and he resumes his reverie on the floor. First staged in 1953, this short work – it lasts a mere 13 minutes – is in the repertory of New York City Ballet, The Royal Ballet, and of the Paris Opéra.

Bottom Jean Guizerix as the Tsar and Dominique Khalfouni as his bride in Yury Grigorovich's *Ivan the Terrible* as staged by the Paris Opéra Ballet in 1976. Yury Grigorovich, chief choreographer of the Moscow Bolshoy Ballet, had created *Ivan the Terrible* in Moscow in 1975 and like his previous *Spartacus*, it is a vast panorama of dancing dealing with an historical subject; in this case the 16th century Tsar who did so much to unify Russia. The ballet shows the tragic events that earned Ivan his title of 'the Terrible': his fights against rebellious noblemen, his love for the beautiful Princess Anastasia, her murder by the nobles, and the awful vengeance that Ivan took upon them. All this made for highly theatrical scenes which utilized the marvellous strength of the male dancers of the company, and the artists of the Paris Opéra were outstandingly good in every demand that Grigorovich made upon them.

Top right Dancers of the Paris Opéra in Maurice Béjart's version of *The Firebird*. Just as Robbins up-dated the ideas of Nijinsky's *Faun*, so Maurice Béjart had the idea of re-interpreting another Diaghilev score: Igor Stravinsky's *The Firebird*. Instead of the magical world of Russian Fairy tale, Béjart is concerned with the Firebird as the symbol of revolutionary fervour. The cast comprises a group of partisans, whose endeavours are inspired by the Firebird, now a male role, which represents the ideas of a human spirit struggling against oppression. This presentation, typical of Béjart, appeals to a youthful audience more interested in its theme than in its choreographic merits. Illustrated are Michaël Denard as the Firebird and Jean-Pierre Franchetti as the partisan leader.

Centre right Maurice Béjart in his own *La Nuit Obscure* with Maria Casarès. In 1970 Maurice Béjart staged a work in three parts — *A la recherche de* . . . . . . (*In search of* . . . . . .) of which the central section involved the declamation of texts by St John of the Cross. Béjart himself appeared in this, together with the celebrated actress Maria Casarès. The illustration shows the moment when Béjart, on the left, has assumed the fantastic costume previously worn by Mme Casarès.

Below The Ballet du XXme Siècle in *Trionfi*. In 1974 Maurice Béjart was invited to create a work inspired by the work and life of the Italian Renaissance poet Petrarch, whose 600th anniversary occurred that year. In the Boboli Gardens of Florence Béjart staged one of his most extravagantly decorative spectacles: *Trionfi* takes its ideas from Petrarch's poems, and was a work filled with exciting visual effects.

There are ballet companies today in France associated with the opera houses or municipal theatres in several important towns, but probably the most interesting development of recent years has been the opening of *Maisons de la Culture* (art complexes) in the French regions. At Amiens, in northern France, the Maison de la Culture was made the home of the *Ballet-Théâtre Contemporain*, founded in 1968. The company was dedicated to the policy of presenting brand new ballets with modern scores and designs by some of the most interesting contemporary artists. Its director, Jean-Albert Cartier, and its choreographic director, Françoise Adret, soon gave the company a vivid modern image. In 1972 the company transferred to Angers, where it now has its base, and continues its distinguished creativity. In the south of France, Roland Petit has recently taken over the direction of the Marseille Ballet, and for this company he has also staged several interesting works, while also continuing to choreograph elsewhere.

It was from Marseille that there came a remarkable choreographer, Maurice Béjart, who trained at the Opéra there, and then toured throughout Europe as a dancer. In 1960, following the success of a work he had staged in Brussels, he was invited to become director of the ballet company at the Théâtre de la Monnaie, Brussels. This company he soon transformed into the Ballet of the Twentieth Century (Le Ballet du XXme Siècle). As its name implies, it is dedicated to the presentation of spectacular modern works. It is also a phenomenon of our time. Using a large company of admirably trained dancers, Béjart stages his works in circus tents and sports stadia as well as theatres, to vast and enthusiastic audiences. In Mexico City he has played to 25,000 people at one time; in West Berlin, he had nightly audiences of 12,000. Wherever the company performs, they are ecstatically received by a predominantly youthful public. While his treatment of his chosen themes may divide critical opinion (he is either adored or loathed by the press in many countries) it must be said that he reaches a vast public who might not otherwise be aware of dance. His ballets can deal with a variety of subjects: *Nijinsky, Clown of God* sought to explain the reasons for Nijinsky's madness; *Golestan* was inspired by Persia; *Bhakti* by Hinduism. His presentations are conceived on a monumental scale: detail is often missing, but there is a broad, simple view which appeals to his audience, and the stagings are often excitingly vital in their massed effects. His school, *Mudra*, in Brussels, attracts students from all over the world.

Above Dancers of the Hamburg State Opera Ballet Company in John Neumeier's *Third Symphony*. One of John Neumeier's major works, this ballet is set to Mahler's third symphony.

Left Dancers of the Ballet-Théâtre Con-temporain in *Hymnen*. This is one of the most adventurous French companies, noted for the particular emphasis it places upon design. No less than five choreographers joined in the creation of *Hymnen* in 1971, which makes use of a score based on the national anthems by the modern composer Karl-Heinz Stockhausen. The brilliant décor by Gérard Fromanger carries out the idea of national flags in which the red has run like blood. *Hymnen* tells something of the aggression that men show under the banner of nationalism. It is a typical product of the company in its interesting use of music, dance and design.

GERMANY, AUSTRIA, ITALY

It is curious that, despite the number of distinguished ballet-masters and dancers who worked in Germany during the 18th and 19th centuries, there has been no continuing tradition of ballet in Germany. During the 1920s and 1930s a form of Modern Dance generally known as the 'Central European' style flourished, especially in the work of Mary Wigman (1886–1973) which reflected the turbulence of the times. There was also Kurt Jooss (b 1901) whose Ballets Jooss based at Essen (and later at Dartington Hall, Devon) toured the world with great success during the 1930s. His best-known work, still in the repertory of several companies, was *The Green Table*, an allegory about war and the cynicism of politicians. The Jooss style, a mixture of comparatively simple, 'free' choreography and forceful, dramatic mime, belonged to the movement that was known as Expressionist theatre – all symbolism and social comment – but it must be looked upon as one of the backwaters of ballet.

After the Second World War, a great change came about. The example of visiting ballet companies inspired a new interest in classical dance. Although there is no national company in West Germany, many cities maintain a ballet company attached to their opera house, and the dancers besides appearing in operas have the opportunity to give occasional evenings of ballet. By far the most celebrated company is that in Stuttgart. It came to prominence following the arrival of John Cranko to revive his full-length *Prince of the Pagodas* there in 1961. Cranko inspired the company, and under his guidance it achieved international renown. This was in part due to Cranko's discovery of Marcia Haydee as his ballerina. Haydee (b 1939) is a Brazilian dancer, trained at the Royal Ballet School, where her contemporaries included Lynn Seymour and Antoinette Sibley. Under Cranko's direction Haydee emerged as a superlative dramatic ballerina, ideal for classic roles as well as those Cranko was to make for her in a number of exciting ballets. In addition Cranko had acquired several other fine principals: Ray Barra (b 1930), and later Richard Cragun (b 1944) and Egon Madsen (b 1942). The repertory that he created had considerable range, from classic, plotless ballets to high comedy and a series of full-length works: *Onegin, Romeo and Juliet, The Taming of the Shrew, Carmen*, as well as a revival of *Swan Lake*: which aroused enormous public interest in Stuttgart and later round the world. Within a short time Cranko's choreographies and the enthusiastic loyalty he aroused in his dancers had gained the Stuttgart company international success.

Cranko's long training with the Royal Ballet had taught him the importance of a school (the Stuttgart Ballet School is one of the finest in Europe today) and also the importance of the continuity of the classic style. Marcia Haydee and Richard Cragun, Egon Madsen and the first true German ballerina, Birgit Keil (a product of Stuttgart),

and the roster of fine soloists who joined the company, brought the Stuttgart Ballet to a pre-eminent position in West Germany. Cranko died in the aeroplane bringing the Stuttgart Ballet back from a triumphant season in New York in 1973. Despite this tragic loss, it is the measure of the organization he had built and the tremendous company loyalty, to him and what he had created, that the company has continued to flourish. It was directed for a year after Cranko's death by Glen Tetley, who also composed some fine ballets for it, but since 1976 the company has been under the guidance of Marcia Haydee.

There are several other notable companies in West Germany, attached to the Opera Houses – those of Deutsche Oper am Rhein, directed by Erich Walter; the company of the Deutsche Oper in West Berlin; companies in Wuppertal and Munich. Their work is often interesting but they have as yet hardly achieved international status. Rather more significant is the work of the American born choreographer John Neumeier (b 1942) who danced for some years with the Stuttgart Ballet before eventually becoming director of the Hamburg Ballet in 1973. Neumeier is a man of brilliant theatrical ideas, and his stagings in Hamburg, and earlier in Frankfurt, where he was director from 1969 to 1973, have excited a great deal of interest. With such productions as *Romeo and Juliet*, *Meyerbeer-Schumann*, *Don Juan*, *Illusions – like Swan Lake* he has won a very high reputation in Germany.

Somewhat similar to Germany, in that it was an important centre of ballet during the 18th and 19th centuries, Vienna has also suffered from the lack of a continuous ballet tradition. Today the Vienna State Ballet, while it maintains a large company, makes little creative contribution to the art.

It is interesting to note that in those countries of Europe where, during the 18th century, opera was very popular and continued to be so during the 19th and 20th centuries, ballet has inevitably become the poor and neglected relation. This is true of Germany, Austria and Italy with their unrivalled operatic traditions: in each country ballet has taken second place at best, existing mostly to feed the opera productions with dancers needed in brief ballet scenes. In Italy, as in Germany and Austria, there are ballet companies associated with the opera houses. At La Scala Milan during the 19th century there was still an attempt made to stage important dance works, and the school attached to the theatre has long produced performers of exceptional technical brilliance (witness those virtuoso ballerinas who so amazed the Russian Imperial Ballet at the end of the last century). But in modern times ballet in Italy – in Rome as well as Milan, which are the two chief centres of dance – has declined: there has been too little attempt to give either continuity or real development to the companies associated with the opera-house. A few exceptionally gifted Italian dancers have become known internationally; among them Elisabetta Terabust (b 1946); Carla Fracci (b 1936) and Paolo Bortoluzzi (b 1938) are much admired for their appearances with the major international companies.

DENMARK AND SWEDEN

Despite the glorious tradition established by August Bournonville, there was no choreographer to succeed him. Bournonville died in 1879, and two days before his death he saw the debut of a young dancer, Hans Beck (b 1861), who was not to die until 1952. Beck, though not a choreographer of much importance, ensured that the repertory of ballets by Bournonville was properly maintained, as well as the teaching system established by that great master. Although during the 1920s and 1930s certain famous choreographers – Fokine, Balanchine – worked with the company briefly, the Royal Danish Ballet tended almost to be a museum of Bournonville works. During the 1930s it found a distinguished native choreographer in Harald Lander (1905–1971) who created an interesting new repertory, but when the Royal Danish Ballet eventually decided to come out into the world, and undertake a first tour in 1954, it was the beauties of the Bournonville ballets – like *La Sylphide*, *A Folk Tale*, *Napoli*, and the magnificence of the dancers trained in the Bournonville school – which excited immense public admiration. Exposed to the world, the Danes decided that they must try and modernize their ballet. One of the greatest teachers, Vera Volkova (1904–1975), a pupil of A. Y. Vaganova, went to Copenhagen to develop the training system in the Royal Danish Ballet. A young dancer, Flemming Flindt (b 1936), was appointed director and chief choreographer, and he set about staging a series of daringly innovative ballets such as *The Lesson*, *The Triumph of Death* and *The Young Man must Marry* which were in violent contrast to the company's Bournonville traditions. Other celebrated choreographers also worked with the company, Ashton, MacMillan and Robbins among them; and today the Royal Danes are held in affectionate esteem throughout the world. It is significant that many companies now try to present Bournonville ballets: they are in the main unsuccessful because of the difficulty of acquiring the genuine Bournonville style which needs training from childhood to assimilate. Great Danish dancers – especially male dancers – have gone out into the world to make magnificent careers: outstandingly is Erik Bruhn (b 1928), hailed as the purest classical stylist of his generation, and Peter Martins (b 1946) who has danced for nearly ten years with the New York City Ballet and is among today's most elegant and powerful *premiers danseurs*. One Danish ballerina, Toni Lánder (b 1931), made an exceptional international career, dancing with London Festival Ballet and then with American Ballet Theatre, to great acclaim.

Like the Russian companies of today, the Royal Danish Ballet also excels in producing outstanding character dancers. Its old repertory relies very much upon the service of senior artists who undertake the dramatic supporting roles, and in any production of a Bournonville ballet like *Napoli* or *The Life Guards on Amager*, much of the pleasure in watching the piece lies in the dramatic portrayals by the senior artists of the company.

SWEDEN

Although the Royal Swedish Ballet was founded as early as 1773, there was no great choreographer or teacher like Bournonville to establish a solid basis of repertory and to ensure a continuity of style. The ballet maintained a rather thin existence for over a century – the most interesting Swedish efforts in ballet being made by the short-lived and independent Ballets Suédois of the early 1920s which was set up to emulate the modernity of Diaghilev. With the ballet boom that followed the end of the Second World War, the English teacher and producer Mary Skeaping (b 1902) became director of the Royal Swedish Ballet for a decade from 1953 to 1962, and produced several fine revivals of the 19th century Russian classics. Various other foreign choreographers, including Tudor and MacMillan have worked in Stockholm, but the company has not known the success of its Danish neighbour. Two other companies in Sweden must be mentioned: the Cullberg Ballet is directed by the choreographer Birgit Cullberg (b 1908) and is dedicated to presenting her ballets; the Gothenberg Ballet was for some years directed by Elsa Marianne von Rosen (b 1927), a Swedish dancer and choreographer who has made some interesting restagings of Bournonville ballets as well as creating her own works.

Below left Niels Kehlet in *Etudes* with the Royal Danish Ballet. In 1948 the Danish choreographer Harald Lander had the clever idea of showing something of the ardours of ballet training by taking a daily class as the basis for a display of dance virtuosity. From the first gentle steps at the barre (see chapter five) to the final fireworks of the most daring steps in the dance vocabulary, the ballet gathers momentum and excitement. As an accompaniment Lander uses the piano exercises of Carl Czerny, known to every piano student, in an orchestration by Knudage Riisager. The illustration shows one of the greatest Danish dancers of today, Niels Kehlet, in a typically soaring leap. The ballet is also in the repertory of London Festival Ballet and the Paris Opéra.

Bottom Mea Venema and Jon Benoit in Jírì Kyliân's *La Cathedrale Engloutie* with the Nederlands Dans Theater. Using Debussy's piano prelude which gives the ballet its title, the Czech-born choreographer Jírì Kyliân – who danced for some years with the Stuttgart Ballet – made a sequence of dances for two couples in 1975, to explore the troubled relationship that exists between them.

Below Dancers of the Royal Danish Ballet in Bournonville's *Le Conservatoire*. In the only surviving scene from this ballet, Bournonville recreated the ballet classes he knew as a student in Paris during the 1820s. Here for the first time is a scene in which a choreographer uses dance training as the basis for an entertainment. See also *Etudes* and *School of Ballet*. The most recent example is Robert Cohen's *Class* for the London Contemporary Dance Theatre which puts the basis of Graham training on stage.

Right Dancers of the Nederland Dans Theater in *Huescape* by Louis Falco. The wide-ranging repertory of the Nederlands Dans Theater has frequently incorporated the work of the most controversial young American choreographers. Among them is Louis Falco, several of whose recent ballets have involved dancers speaking as well as such unusual properties as giant plastic sturgeons, and a large pile of feathers. *Huescape*, however, an early work, is more conventional and deals with the age-old battle for affection between three people.

HOLLAND

With no classical traditions worthy of note before the Second World War, there was a surprising and unexpected interest in ballet in the post-war years. This eventually led, through the work of various dancers, choreographers and teachers, to the establishment of the two main companies in Holland: The National Ballet and the Nederlands Dans Theater. The National Ballet came into being in 1961, as the amalgamation of two existing troupes. The company is large and its repertory wide ranging: classical stagings and modern creativity exist side by side. Nederlands Dans Theater was founded in 1959, and its prolific schedule of new ballets attracted world attention: each year some ten or more creations are staged, many of them highly experimental. Chief among its choreographers at one time was Hans van Manen (b 1932), the foremost Dutch ballet-maker, and he composed a series of very effective works for the company, some of which were later to enter the repertory of major European companies – the Royal Ballet has no less than 6 of his works.

Hans van Manen then went on to work with the Dutch National Ballet, where he joined two other choreographers – Rudi van Dantzig (b 1933) and Toer van Schayk (b 1936). All three have maintained a constant stream of new works for the company, many of them somewhat controversial. Nederlands Dans Theater has – like Ballet Rambert – owned much to the influence of the work of Glen Tetley, who for a time was director of the company. Latterly it suffered from the injection of too many pretentious American dance ideas, which sapped it of its real identity, but now under the directorship of Jiří Kylián it is rediscovering its original character.

A third Dutch company, which has contributed considerably to the national interest in the art, is the Scapino Ballet, which tours throughout the country giving performances for school audiences.

It is interesting to note that, in contrast to all the other major national companies in Europe, the Dutch are alone in not having a school directly linked to their companies.

EASTERN EUROPE

At the end of the war in 1945, when much of Eastern Europe fell under the dominance of the Soviet Union, countries such as Latvia, Poland, Hungary, Rumania, Bulgaria, Czechoslovakia, and the rather more independent Yugoslavia, all set about developing their ballet companies. In Poland, there was a long balletic heritage; and in many of the others there is a strong and vital interest in folk-dance as a means of expression. The ballet troupes and schools established in these countries after the war have received considerable encouragement and practical help from the Soviet Union, but much of their work remains unknown in the West.

CANADA, AUSTRALIA, SOUTH AFRICA

The flourishing national ballets in Canada and Australia are direct descendants of the Royal Ballet. The Canadian National Ballet was founded by Celia Franca who went to Canada at the suggestion of Dame Ninette de Valois after the Royal Ballet's first triumphant tour of North America in 1949. For 20 years Celia Franca had to work tremendously hard to sustain the growth of her company, and in this she was aided by the presence of the outstanding National Ballet School in Toronto, under the direction of Betty Oliphant. The National School is one of the finest we know, and its graduates now form the major part of the National Ballet's ensemble: outstanding are Karen Kain, Frank Augustyn, Nadia Potts, Veronica Tennant and Mary Jago. The style and repertory of the company are recognizably linked with that of the Royal Ballet, but the Canadians' freshness of manner and their youthful charm are especially their own. Canada has not yet found a major choreographer, but the National Ballet, like the Royal Ballet, maintains a strong classical repertory; its dancers are extremely impressive, and in recent years it has toured abroad with great success. The special relationship with the Royal Ballet has been continued with the appointment of Alexander Grant (b 1925) as Director in 1976. Grant, a character dancer of genius, joined the Sadler's Wells School as a scholar from New Zealand in 1946, and thereafter rose to become a principal of the company and created many important roles – unforgettably, Alain in Ashton's *La Fille mal Gardée*.

For an enormous country, which still remains relatively under-populated, Canada maintains several other companies: The Grands Ballets Canadiens, The Royal Winnipeg Ballet, and several experimental modern groups.

In Australia a somewhat similar situation exists. The Ballets Russes of the 1930s toured Australia, as did Pavlova, but it was the work of Edouard Borovansky (1902–1959) (a Ballet Russe dancer who settled in Australia) who did much to encourage a public interest in ballet during the 1940s and '50s. His company disbanded in 1960 and its members

Top left John Meehan, Gail Ferguson and Ross Stretton in Sir Robert Helpmann's ballet *Perisynthyon* for the Australian Ballet.

Above Artists of the National Ballet of Canada in Gerald Arpino's *Kettentanz* (Chain Dances).

Above left Marilyn Rowe, John Meehan, Gary Norman and Alida Chase in Glen Tetley's *Gemini* for the Australian Ballet.

Top centre Lucette Aldous as Kitri in Act 1 of Rudolf Nureyev's staging of *Don Quixote* for the Australian Ballet.

Top Marilyn Rowe as the Merry Widow in Act 1 of Ronald Hynd's danced version of the celebrated Lehar operetta. The production was devised and staged for the Australian ballet by Sir Robert Helpmann.

were the nucleus of the Australian Ballet which was founded two years later. Under the direction of Dame Peggy van Praagh (who had directed the Sadler's Wells Theatre Ballet for many years) the new young company quickly established itself. In 1965 the Australian-born dancer and choreographer Sir Robert Helpmann joined Dame Peggy in directing the company, and for them he produced a number of ballets. Like their Canadian contemporaries, the Australian dancers were given the benefit of a fine school and the existence of sound classical stagings in the company repertory. Rudolf Nureyev staged *Don Quixote* and *Raymonda* for them (just as he had mounted *The Sleeping Beauty* for the Canadian company).

The Australian Ballet has toured internationally with great success: visiting Poland and Russia in 1973, as well as Britain on three occasions. Its principals include Lucette Aldous (who danced with the Royal Ballet, Ballet Rambert and Festival Ballet as ballerina before going to Australia), Kelvin Coe, Marilyn Jones, John Meehan, and a strong group of soloists. In 1976, Anne Woolliams (b 1926) was appointed director of the company. She had previously been ballet-mistress in Stuttgart during John Cranko's directorate of the ballet there. Australia also numbers several small ensembles which produce new work and tour throughout the vastness of the continent.

In South Africa the Royal Ballet's influence is less direct. The country has produced many fine dancers – notably Nadia Nerina (b 1927), who became a leading ballerina of the Royal Ballet and was the original Lise in *La Fille mal Gardée*, Maryon Lane and John Cranko. The work of an outstanding teacher, Dulcie Howes, in Cape Town, did much to stimulate public interest in ballet, and the establishment of a ballet company on the Cape developed from her school. This is the CAPAB Ballet, which is now directed by yet another one-time Royal Ballet principal, David Poole (b 1925). The PACT Ballet, like CAPAB, is based in Johannesburg in the Transvaal, and is also a classical company. The permanent troupe has been host to a series of very celebrated guests, from Dame Margot Fonteyn, Natalya Makarova and Anthony Dowell to Sir Frederick Ashton and Sir Robert Helpmann (who appeared as the Ugly Sisters in Ashton's *Cinderella*).

Elsewhere throughout the world, ballet and dance flourish as never before. From Japan to Norway, from South Africa to South America, in China and Cuba, there is a continuing and developing interest in dance. This world-wide interest in the art has meant that performers and dance students travel long distances in search of fine teaching or of engagements: there is a true internationalism now apparent in dance, and during any year in the major centres of ballet – New York, London, Paris, Moscow – dancers from all parts of the globe will be found at work.

This section of the book is intended to give some insight into the daily work of the dancer, both as student and as a professional member of a ballet company. It owes everything to the guidance and knowledge of Miss Maryon Lane, a principal dancer of the Royal Ballet until her retirement in 1969, who is now a teacher at the Royal Ballet School. Through the courtesy of Mr Michael Wood, Director of the Royal Ballet School, and Miss Barbara Fewster, Principal of the Royal Ballet School, we have been fortunate in being able to use Miss Briony Brind and Mr Paul Tomkinson, first year students in the Upper School, as models for the pictures which were specially taken by Anthony Crickmay for this book. Miss Lane, who danced many of the leading roles in the Royal Ballet's repertory, both classical and contemporary, has provided all the technical descriptions and guidance for this section. We would also like to record our grateful thanks to Mr Terence Newman, C.B.E., for invaluable help.

GUIDE TO CLASSICAL BALLET STEPS

This section cannot give a complete analysis of a ballet class. It is impossible to illustrate much of the work because so many of the dancers' studies are in detailed movement which cannot be adequately recorded even in a series of pictures. Nevertheless, we have tried to suggest something of the immense care and thought that must go into the training of a dancer in the classic academic style that has been developed over several centuries. Because of its origins in France, the vocabulary of steps still remains in the French language, and has been retained here with simple English translations. We must also stress here that the exercises have been shown only on 'one side' ie the dancers are seen working only in one direction. It must be realized, of course, that all exercises at the barre, and in the centre of the class room, are given alternately on one leg and then on the other.

Far left Maris Liepa of the Bolshoy Ballet in a *grand jeté* from the pas de deux in the last act of *The Sleeping Beauty*. This leap, by one of the Bolshoy Ballet's leading dancers, exemplifies all those basic qualities that are continually emphasised in class.

Above Vladimir Gelvan of the Bolshoy Ballet leaping in an exciting *temps de poisson* during a performance of *School of Ballet*. This is a divertissement devised by Asaf Messerer, a great Russian teacher and ballet master, in which he displays all the excitement and aspirations of ballet training. It is a theatricalisation of daily class, and like class it builds to a wonderful climax of virtuosity.

Left Irina Kolpakova as Princess Florine in the third act of *The Sleeping Beauty* with the Leningrad State Kirov Ballet. Kolpakova has the purest classical style, and the harmony of line in this *attitude* from the Bluebird pas de deux is evidence of what the Vaganova system of training is capable of achieving.

THE PULL-UP AND THE TURN-OUT

In ballet there are two essential and initial technical requirements; the pull-up and the turn-out. It is important for a dancer to stand as tall as possible. The back should be straight and the feeling is that the top of the head is reaching for the ceiling, resulting in an uplift throughout the body. The stomach muscles are firm and the body is well lifted off the hips, thus encouraging a beautifully slim waist. The dancer, like the singer and actor, has to breathe easily and deeply from the diaphragm using the lower ribs which expand sideways. A good, steady supply of oxygen is needed to ensure that all the muscles work well.

The turn-out is the placing of the legs, which are turned from the hip-sockets. Ideally, mostly after many years of work, a dancer gains a 90° turn-out; ie since the toes normally face the front, in a 90° turn-out the toes face the sides (1). It is important that the placing begins at the top of the legs in the hip-sockets and not in the knees or ankles, which would put far too much strain on these joints and might well result in injuries. The turn-out makes the line of the legs and feet very beautiful and, strangely enough, it makes all the dancer's work far easier because it gives extra strength to the movements.

PORT DE BRAS

Port de bras means the carriage of the arms. As the legs and feet have their correct positioning so have the arms and hands. Every part of the dancer's body is disciplined to form correct and pleasing lines – very much like the pianist's scales. When the correct rules from the fingers through to the toes have been learned thoroughly then the dancer can truly begin to dance. The arms are held always without tension; the elbows are always slightly bent so as to maintain a flowing unbroken line. As the pull-up is designed to make a dancer appear to be very long and tall, so the positions of the arms are based on achieving the same effect. Ballet is so much illusion; even a small dancer can look tall when all these techniques are used to their full. The elbows therefore never break the line of the arm, neither do the wrists, and the fingers also should feel long and extended, and yet be placed gently. The middle finger is the absolute end of the arm and the dancer should be conscious of a continuous and yet very slightly rounded line right through the arm to the tip of the middle finger.

HEAD AND EYES

With all the technical training of a dancer's limbs it is important not to forget the head and eyes. The eyes reflect the dancer's thoughts and changes of mood depending on the movements or the rôle to be played. Normally, especially during the barre exercises it can be seen how the head is held on a beautifully long neck, with no tension in the upper back and neck-muscles. The eyes focus naturally at the eye-level and see from the centre of the face. The eyes can become strained and many young students can be seen to be gazing tensely into space or at the ceiling, and yet not really looking. The eyes must look out calmly and be aware of what they are looking at. The importance of the eyes and head in all forms of pirouettes will be discussed later.

THE POSITIONS

1 FIRST POSITION (1)

The heels are together and the legs and feet at 90° turn-out. The body is long and well-lifted. The arms are beautifully curved and the fingers are only a few inches apart. The weight is evenly balanced on both legs.

2 SECOND POSITION (2)

The feet are approximately 1½ times the length of the dancer's foot apart. The arms in the second position slope down from the shoulders and form one long curve down to the middle finger of the hands. Notice that the elbows did not drop and therefore are not angular; likewise the hand and wrist are in alignment – thus we achieve one long continuous curve without any broken lines. Again there is the feeling of length, as though the arms and hands are far longer than they really are. Notice the ease of the arms and the lack of strain. The palms of the hands face front.

3 THIRD POSITION (3)

The heel of one foot is placed close to the middle of the other foot. This position is easier to obtain than the fifth position; it is used very much in the training of younger dancers because it does not require quite the strength in the turn-out as the fifth position. The arms are in third position as well, ie one arm in the first position and one in the second.

4 FOURTH POSITION (4)

There are two fourth positions. The easier (fourth *ouverte* – French, open) is obtained by one foot going directly forward by about 12″ from the first position; again as with the third position it is taught to younger dancers because it does not require quite so much strength; but here you see illustrated the fourth *croisée* (French – crossed), always used by stronger dancers able to hold the turn-out of the legs, with one foot going directly forward by about 12″ from the fifth position. The arms are again held with *slightly* curved elbows forming a pleasing line with no tension in the arm. The weight is evenly placed on both legs.

3   4   5

9   10   11

5 FIFTH POSITION (5)

The feet are well 'crossed' so that they are exactly behind each other; the toe of one behind the heel of the other. The arms in their long curve, with the palms of the hands facing each other, allow the fingers softly stretched to complete the line.

BARRE WORK

The class work always begins at the barre. The barre should be placed so that the dancer can hold it at approximately waist level without distorting the shoulders. The barre is necessary to aid the dancer in the daily preparation of class but it should never be held tightly. So often a tightly-held hand on the barre means the dancer is working very much off-balance. The barre is there as a guide but the dancer has to be conscious of standing firmly over his or her own feet and make sure not to be using the arms to pull on the barre to keep balance.

During the barre exercises the slow preparation of the muscles takes place, warming them, stretching them gently, preparing them for the greater demands that are to be made when the dancer moves into the centre to work and the minimal support provided by the barre is no longer available.

PLIÉS

6 *Pliés* (French *plier* – to bend) (6, 7) start the class to
7 encourage mobility and help turn-out and the placing of the body. The correct placing – the 90°-turn-out – may take years of training to achieve. In a *plié* the aim is to bend the legs, from whichever of the five positions is the starting-point, without straining the muscles. The knees go out over the middle toes of the corresponding foot, until the thighs are horizontal. In the closed positions (first, third and fifth) the heels are allowed to rise; in the open positions the heels must be kept on the floor. In

pictures 6 and 7 Briony is performing a *plié* in the first position and Paul in second. At the start of a *plié* the dancer stands tall. The whole spine is stretched and straight. As the knees start to bend there is no tension in the muscles of the legs, the movement is slow and careful. Notice in the pictures how the body remains well pulled-up and the waist firm. The back remains straight whilst the dancer concentrates on turning out from the top of the legs. As a dancer comes up from the *plié* the muscles in the top of the legs and thighs begin their work of sustaining the turn-out. At the same time it is important to remember that the whole body must be co-ordinated. In the pictures one arm is placed lightly on the barre, while the working arm moves from second position down to what is known as *bras bas* (French – low arm), its lowest curved position, as in picture 7. The eyes follow the hand as the arm is moved, looking beyond it; then the arm is returned through first position to second, the eyes continuing to look beyond the hand. Although this is an exercise it is the beginning of a *dance* class and the eyes and head must be used in harmony.
Demi-plié (French *demi* – half). This movement is exactly what it is called: a half-*plié*. However, a dancer never goes so far down into the movement as to allow the heels to rise from the floor in the closed positions (ie first, third and fifth). The *demi-plié* is used constantly as a preparation to the majority of steps, such as before pirouettes, before rising on to three-quarter point or full point and before jumps. This applies to all steps provided the movement starts on two feet; a *demi-plié* movement performed on one leg is very similar to a *fondu*, (see below).

TENDUS

8 *Tendu* (French *tendre* – to stretch) (8, 9, 10). *Tendus*
9 are shown to the front (8), to the side (9), to the back
10 (10). From *pliés* the class proceeds to *tendus*.

The *tendu* starts from fifth position, the body as always held erect but at ease. It is a stretching of the leg and foot, well turned-out, in which one leg slides forward, sideways, or back, without lifting the toes from the floor. The weight of the body is on the supporting leg, and the body is held in a perfectly straight line as can be seen in the pictures. The movement is begun by the heel and finally continued by the toes.

We must now consider the work of the foot and toes. The dancer has to be conscious always that when standing on the feet the toes are long and flat; the toes should not curl and grip the floor. The stronger muscles in the leg and body should be playing their part in holding the dancer's weight and allowing the foot to feel long and stretched underneath the toes. If the dancer's weight is well on the supporting leg it should not be necessary for the toes to grip and curl in trying to hold the dancer on balance. As the working leg goes into *tendu* the foot is strongly arched but again the toes are kept stretched and long; they must not be allowed to curl over.

GLISSÉS

11 *Glissé* (French *glisser* – to glide) (11). In the slow exercises of *tendu* the toes are kept on the floor, in *glissé* the foot is slightly lifted off the ground, some two to three inches. This ensures later on that whenever the feet are off the ground they are meticulously pointed, the purpose being to develop a swift foot reaction which is essential for preparing for *allegro* (quick) work.

As with *tendus*, dancers do *glissés* to the front (French – *devant*), to the side (*à la seconde*) in second position, and behind (*derrière*). A succession of steps carried out in this order is called *en croix* (French – in the form of a cross).

12

13

14

18

19

20

21

22

Barre Work (continued)

FONDUS

12 *Fondus* (French *fondre* – to melt) (12, 13, 14). The
13 class is gradually preparing to raise the working
14 foot and leg higher and higher from the floor as
these muscles are warmed up. This is an important
exercise. It develops the strength of the supporting
leg which carries the weight of the body throughout
the movement. The supporting leg is trained to carry
the weight of the body as the knees bend and then
straighten again. It is invaluable for preparing jumps
when a dancer has to push up through the supporting
leg from the *fondu*, bending the knee, to a straight
leg, and to land once more gently through the foot.
No-one should prepare a jump nor land from it with
straight knees. The starting position is shown in
picture 12 where the two dancers' right feet are seen
'*sur le cou de pied*' (French – on the neck of the foot),
with the working foot placed with the little toe just
above the ankle-bone of the supporting leg. The *cou
de pied* position can be in front (for the *fondu devant*),
or *à la seconde*, or behind (for the *fondu derrière*). In
the position behind it is the big toe which is placed
just above the ankle-bone. In picture 13 both the
supporting and working legs are moving towards

the straightened position; in picture 14 the movement is complete, with the working leg extended
forward and the foot fully stretched. The exercise
must be smoothly and slowly done.

RONDS DE JAMBE A TERRE

Ronds de Jambe à Terre (French – circling of the leg
15 on the ground) (15). This is an exercise used to help
the turn-out at the hip-socket. The leg describes a
semi-circle, moving through a *tendu* to the front,
side, and back before closing in first position. The
picture shows a *rond de jambe à terre* at its extension to
the side. The toe never leaves the floor and the foot is
always fully stretched and the leg turned out. As the
foot returns to the first position the heel is brought
down and the foot and toes fully stretched on the
floor.

FRAPPÉS

16 *Frappés* (French *frapper* – to strike) (16). The position
is shown with the dancers on three-quarter pointe,
with the foot flexed (not pointed), in the *cou de pied*.
The exercise is performed in sharp accents, working
from the knee down to the foot. The lower leg is
extended in second position, with the foot fully
pointed, and is brought back to the *cou de pied* of the
supporting leg. The exercise, which can also be

performed to the front and back develops the flexibility of ankle, knee and foot, and is performed
quickly and cleanly.

RONDS DE JAMBE EN L'AIR

Ronds de jambe en l'air (French – circling of the leg
17 in the air) (17). It is important to note here that not
only is the leg being increasingly raised in exercises,
but also a variety of exercises ensures that all the
different muscles of the leg are brought equally into
play, so that none is over-worked.

The leg is placed in second position, describes an
oval shape in the air, reaches a *retiré* (French – drawn-
up) position with the big toe placed at the side of the
knee, and returns to the extended second position
and is closed in fifth position. In the picture Briony
is demonstrating the *retiré* position and Paul shows
the *rond de jambe en l'air* at its fullest extent to the
side. The movement is done both *en dehors* (ie in an
outwards direction) and *en dedans* (inwards). The
exercise is important in that not only does it help
the dancer to hold the raised thigh in its fully
turned-out position and to keep the hips level, but
the upper body still, but it stresses mobility from the
knee. This is a taxing exercise, and the pace is eased
by following it with a small, quick exercise for
beaten steps.

15

16

17

23

24

25

26

PETITS BATTEMENTS

Petit Battement (French *petit* – small; *battement* –
18 beating) (18). This exercise is primarily for *batterie*
(beaten steps). These steps are mainly known for the
brilliant and quick changing of the position of the
ankles and feet in mid-air. A notable example is the
entrechat, in which the dancer jumps into the air and
rapidly crosses and changes the pointed feet from
back to front in fifth position *en l'air*, the legs
extended. The 'beating' is done with the lower part
of the calves. Each change of the leg position counts
as two *entrechats*, as the dancer is using both legs.
Hence dancers are spoken of as beating *entrechat
quatre* (four) with two changes of both legs; *entrechat
six* (six) with three changes of both legs; or exceptionally *entrechat huit* (eight) with four changes of
both legs.

In *petits battements* the heel is very important in that
the foot is brought to the front *cou de pied*, and then
brought back to the *cou de pied* position behind in
varying tempi. In picture 18 Briony demonstrates
the front position of the heel and Paul the position
of the back. This encourages swiftness, so important
in the later *batterie* steps. The concentration is on the
work of the heel of the foot crossing both front and
back; the work is done from the knee, the thigh held
steady and turned-out.

GRANDS BATTEMENTS

19 *Grands Battements* (French *grand* – big) (19, 20, 23).
20 This exercise is used for limbering the legs to gain
23 further extension when the body has been thoroughly
warmed by the preceding work. The leg starts from
the fifth position, moves through *tendu* and *glissé*,
continues to swing through to its maximum height,
without distorting the hip-line or the supporting
leg. It is a preparation for *allegro*, the bright brilliant
work in which the legs must seem light and free in
movement. These *grands battements* are performed
to the front, the side, and the back. (19, 20 show the
battements to the front). When the *battements* are done
to the back the body momentarily stretches forward
to allow the leg to lift for the *arabesque* (see later)
position in picture 23. Notice the long stretch in the
waist line remains.

DEVELOPPES

21 *Développés* (a developing movement) (21–25). These
are steps of *adagio* which means that they are performed at a slow tempo; they are performed only
when the dancer's body is properly warmed up. The
legs are going to be extended to their highest point
but at a slow tempo. In picture 21 Briony is in a
retiré position, viewed from the side: from there she
22 moves into an *attitude* (22) – the thigh is strongly

lifted and in picture 23 the leg is extended from the
knee into *arabesque*. (The *attitude* is a position said to
have been created by the great teacher Carlo Blasis
(1795–1878), inspired by the statue of Mercury by
Giovanni de Bologna (see p 90). Paul is showing the
24 *développé* to the side in pictures 24 and 25, beginning
25 with a *retiré*, then fully extending the leg to the side.

Développés can be performed to the front, the
side, and to the back; the purpose being to develop
control in the unfolding of the leg to its fullest
extent and to show beautiful line. Throughout
these movements the carriage of the torso and the
pulling-up of the abdominal muscles and spine are
essential.

26 LIMBERING (26)
At the end of the barre section of the class the dancers
can spend a moment stretching their bodies by using
the barre for support. The hips are kept square and
the aim is to lengthen the muscles throughout the
leg. Dancers are always aware of how their muscles
are developing: if their work is careful and their
training is correct the proportions of the body are
improved, the muscles becoming long, strong and
supple.

CENTRE WORK

The dancers leave the barre and work in the centre of the floor now that their muscles are properly tuned. It is important to realize the relationship between the two halves of the class; in starting centre work the dancers return to the first barre exercises and now perform them without the slight aid of the barre. Simple *ports de bras* are done, and then perhaps *tendus*, etc. Then concentration is turned on to *pirouettes* (see below) and from this the class becomes increasingly demanding in technical skill. After turning steps (*pirouettes*) can come *adagio*: the importance here is the acquisition of balance through the control which is being built up, and then the development of *allegro*. All of these different qualities of movement are used in a dancer's performance. Balance, line, the use of the various alignments and positions of the body are all vital.

POSITIONS OF THE BODY

27 Croisé devant (French – crossed in front) (27). The front leg is seen placed across the body which is held obliquely; arms are in fourth position.

28 Croisé derrière (French – crossed behind) (28). In this picture Briony has her working leg 'crossed' in the rear in *arabesque*, and her body is placed obliquely: arms are in fourth position.

29 Ecarté devant (French – separated in front) (29). The body is placed obliquely in line with the working leg. Briony is showing the arm and leg position for this movement; notice her head is turned towards the lifted arm.

30 A la seconde (French – in second position) (30). The leg is in second position as are the arms; the body is facing the front.

31 Effacé (French – turned away) (31). The body is held in an open position; the arms are in opposition in fourth position.

32 En face devant (French – directly facing front) (32). All these alignments give colour to dancing by their variety. The illustrated positions of the legs are simple and straightforward and it is the way these positions are enhanced by various alignments and oppositions of the torso and arms which give great interest to the dance. The positions of the arms (*ports de bras*) usually connected with them are shown below (33–36).

33 1st *arabesque* (33), 2nd *arabesque* (34), 3rd *arabesque*
36 (35), *arabesque penché* (36).

27

28

34

33

30

29

32

31

35

36

37

37A

39

40

41

42

38

43

44

45

37 ATTITUDE CROISEE (37)
Paul and Briony are shown in this position which was inspired by the statue of Mercury illustrated next to them (37A).

PIROUETTES

Pirouettes form a necessary part of a class. They are turning steps and can be taken at any tempo, e.g. in adagio work they are in rhythm with the slow, controlled music. However, they are predominantly associated with brilliance and speed, e.g. the famous 32 *fouettés* in *Swan Lake*. (French *fouetter* – to whip: a *fouetté* is a pirouette in which one leg whips round). There are many different ways of starting and ending a *pirouette*. The one perhaps most often seen is a *pirouette* commencing in fourth position (*demi plié*) ending in fifth position (*demi plié*). The arms are usually in first position for this particular *pirouette*.

During the turn, the working leg is lifted almost into a *retiré* position, the little toe of the working leg comes to just under the front of the supporting knee. (In *retiré*, the toes of the working foot come to the side of the supporting knee.)

The head and eyes are of enormous importance in turning. The head is held upright on the spine and the eyes focus on an object that is at eye level. Let us imagine that we are going to do a *pirouette* turning to the right and that, to begin, we are facing the front. The body commences to turn beginning with the shoulders, the eyes and head remain still as long as possible to the front, the eyes still focussing on the same object until the head is well over the left shoulder. At that point it is necessary quickly to turn the head over the right shoulder, bringing the eyes back again to focus again on the same object in front. The body completes the full turn and the shoulders face the front once more.

Pirouettes can be performed in jumping too. The boys do the *double tour en l'air*. They start in fifth position, right foot in front (*demi plié*), spring into the air, complete two circles (changing the feet once) and land back in fifth position (*demi plié*), left foot in front.

PETIT ALLEGRO

38 *Soubresaut* (French – quick jump) (38). A jump from a *demi-plié* in fifth position in which the feet are stretched in fifth position *en l'air* to return in a soft *demi-plié* in fifth position on landing. The feet do not change position; only the front foot ought to show, as demonstrated by Paul and Briony.

Changements de pied (changing of foot positions). All *allegro* jumps begin from two legs, to land on two legs. This step is like a *soubresaut*, except that the feet change position once in the air. The jumping from two legs to two legs ensures that there is no strain on the legs at this time; this is a necessary warming-up process for larger jumps.

PAS DE CHAT

39 *Pas de chat* (French – step of the cat) (39–42). Briony starts from a *demi-plié* in fifth position (39), arms in third position with her head over the curved arm. She jumps to the side, raising the leading leg to a **40** *retiré* position (40); as she begins to descend, the leading leg is extended while the following leg, in turn, **41** is raised to the *retiré* position (41) immediately **42** before landing again in fifth position (42). This is a pretty step, for a girl predominantly – a little pouncing jump – which can be seen often performed by the White Cat in the last act of *The Sleeping Beauty*.

TEMPS DE POISSON

43 *Temps de Poisson* (French literally – a 'fish' leap) (43). The boy springs into the air, arching his body with both arms and legs in immaculate fifth positions. The effect is sleek, like a fish leaping out of the water. It can best be seen in the start of the male dancer's 'Bluebird' variation in the last act of *The Sleeping Beauty*.

BRISE VOLE

44 *Brise volé* (a broken step in the air) (44, 45). In this **45** step the base of the calves are going to beat and the feet cross in the air. This is another step seen in the Bluebird solo. When a step is called *volé* (French *voler* – to fly) it is performed in a travelling jump.

46

47

48

49

50

51

Centre Work (continued)

JETE

46
47
48
Jeté (French *jeter* – to throw. In ballet this means a soaring leap) (46, 47, 48). With the arms extended into fifth position, this tremendous jumping step is seen in picture 46, with Paul's back beautifully held. In picture 47, the line of the arms is in second *arabesque* and the legs are in a *croisé* position. We see here two examples of the great ideal for a male dancer in jumps, which is elevation – the ability to rise high in the air. The complementary quality for dancers is *ballon*, which is the resilience that they show in jumping, their bounce and springiness even in small steps of elevation, like the *soubresaut*, in which a feeling of lightness is needed. In picture 48, we see the feeling of lightness and ease in the girl's jump. Her arms are in third *arabesque* position.

ECHAPPE

49 *Echappé* (French – to escape) (49). The first exercise performed on point, in preparation for the major point work that is to follow in the class. Starting from fifth position in *demi plié*, the legs extend to second position on point and then return to *demi plié* fifth position. The weight is evenly divided over the legs. Before a student attempts point work, she must already have a well-established technique – the earliest age generally accepted for this is 11 years, provided there has been adequate study beforehand. One cannot stress too much the danger that can come from premature use of the points. Tremendous care must be taken in the choosing of point shoes, which must never cramp the toes: the toes must be able to lie flat. Too narrow shoes, and low cut shoes (which offer no support to the toe joints) can harm a young dancer's feet.

50 RETIRE ON POINT (50).
From *échappé* on two feet we move on to work on one foot. The *retiré* (drawn-up) position starts in fifth position *demi-plié*, and the working foot is drawn up to the side of the supporting leg and closes in the fifth position *demi-plié*. The balance is perfectly maintained over the supporting leg. *Retirés* are used as a preparation for *pirouettes*.

51 THE POINT (51)
A strong secure point: the weight is perfectly balanced through the centre-line of each foot (ie the first three toes, commencing with the big toe). There is no *sickling*, in which the foot rolls sickle-like over either big or little toe.

52 POSE ARABESQUE ON POINT (52)
This, of all positions, demonstrates what is meant by good line: the correct placing of the body, the pull-up, the turn-out, and the sense of the body fully but easily stretched, with the head and shoulders naturally and beautifully poised. The whole body is in perfect balance.

PAS DE DEUX (Double Work)

Double work is always taken as a separate class, after both boys and girls have been properly prepared in the general class. The boy and girl must be
53 mutually complementary. In picture 53 we see a simple example in which the boy uses both hands to
54 support the girl. In picture 54 Paul again supports Briony with both arms in *arabesque*: he makes sure she is well-balanced – the pose will be recognized from *Swan Lake* Act 2 *pas de deux*. The male dancer must in *pas de deux* understand how the ballerina's weight is distributed; he must feel not only his own body, but also be aware of how hers is balanced. The male dancer's sensitivity extends to his complete sympathy with his partner's physique: the object in double-work is to display the quality of the ballerina to its very best advantage. If the male dancer is attentive and considerate, the audience will watch him and respect him quite as much as they do the ballerina. The male dancer can make or mar a *pas de deux* by his care for the ballerina or his lack of it. When the ballerina performs *pirouettes*, it is very

52

53

54

important that the male dancer assists her by making sure that she is kept on balance with his hands at her waist: if he is careless he can force her off balance and ruin the dance. The two dancers in *pas de deux* must be in communion; they have to 'give' to each other. Dancers in ballet school start the very early study of double-work by the time they are 14. In

55 picture 55 Paul is supporting Briony in an *attitude*
56 *croisé*, complementing her line. Picture 56 is a 'Fish Dive' in which the girl holds the position of a *temps de poisson*. This pose is seen in the *grand pas de deux* in the last act of *The Sleeping Beauty*. The man places the girl over his leg; he is in a lunge, the girl has performed a *pirouette*, and lands supported across his knee, her leg locked by his arm. It is up to the boy to place the girl very carefully as she lands. In picture

57 57 is seen the final pose of the 'Black Swan' *pas de*
58 *deux* from *Swan Lake* Act III. In picture 58 Maryon Lane is seen correcting Briony, to make sure that her shoulders are in line with her hips and her hips level as she limbers at the barre.

EPAULEMENT

Epaulement ('shouldering': French *épaule* – shoulder)
59 (59). To avoid dancing looking too 'square' and forward facing, the turning of the body – using the body's flexibility from the waist – is employed to give variety. The expressiveness of the body is heightened by the altering of the shoulder positions which gives a flow of movement adding to the quality of dance itself.

55

56

57

58

59

94

PRESERVING BALLETS
By Clement Crisp

It might seem impossible to write down movement. To describe fully and correctly the simplest gesture – like shaking hands with friends – demands reams of words which even then will prove unsatisfactory. Imagine, then, the difficulty of recording a whole ballet involving up to 60 dancers and lasting perhaps three hours in some form of notation. Nevertheless, notation – the idea of 'noting down' movement – is almost as old as European dance history: a first very basic example dates from 1463. Various systems were devised in the 18th and 19th centuries, but all were ultimately unsatisfactory. Those ballets that have been preserved have lasted through a direct transmission of steps and style from one generation of dancers to another. Until very recently, a ballet was preserved, entirely through the efforts of a producer, who – knowing a ballet and its choreography – restaged it for new dancers: and thus the work was in essence preserved, though much small and important detail might be lost.

Forms of notation were useful as aids to memory – we owe our Western staging of the 'classics' to the fact that Nicholas Sergueyev used his notation of the old ballets as a basis for his productions during the 1930s and 1940s. Certain great dancers were also able to reconstruct ballets and, equally important, suggest to new interpreters of the roles the correct 'style' of performance. Even in the age of the cinema, it was not usual to record ballets: there is – unforgiveably – not one inch of film that shows the Diaghilev company in action, and this at a time when the cinema had already created its own classics and preserved many events of world importance on film. It was the system of notation devised by Rudolf von Laban (1879–1958) which created an important step forward, and Labanotation is widely known and used as a recording system of movement. After the war Rudolf Benesh (1916–1975) also invented a system of notation and this is much used by ballet companies today. Other systems also exist and are used: more important as an immediate aid to work is the Video-tape, which makes an instant televisual recording of dancing.

What cannot be replaced by any system of recording yet devised is the 'life' of the dance, which is the choreographer's style and the original dancers' interpretations. Here, the presence of the dancer as teacher and demonstrator is essential: if the image behind a dance – the thought that has coloured its creation and interpretation – is missing, the dance is dead, no matter how careful are the actual mechanics of its revival. A case in point is Fokine's beautiful dance-poem, Le Spectre de la Rose, created for Karsavina and Nijinsky in 1911 and never satisfactorily performed since. The particular qualities that the artists brought to their roles are those which cannot be regained by a mere performing of the steps. Certain ballets should perhaps be allowed to die, and the ghost of what they meant to audiences should be left on the printed page rather than totally dissipated on stage.

INDEX

ACKNOWLEDGMENTS

The publishers would like to thank the following individuals and organizations for their kind permission to reproduce the photographs in this book:

Myra Armstrong 76 below left; BBC Copyright, Photograph by John Green 26 left; Clarke-Crisp Collection 9 left, above and below right, 14 left, 42 above left and right, below left and right, 53 above left; Anthony Crickmay 2–3, 16, 17 above, 18–19, 25, 26–27, 28 left, 30, 31, 32, 34 above, 34–35, 39, 43 above, 44 above and below, 46 above, 46–47 above and below, 47 above and below, 53 above right, 52–53, 53 below, 54–55 above and below, 56 left and right, 57 above left and right, below left and right, 59, 60 left, 60–61 above, 61 above and below, 70–71, 78 above left, 79 right, 80 below left and right, 82 above and below; Amanda Currey 58 above; Jesse Davis 50–51, 64–65, 65, 78 below left; Dominic Photography 4–5, 27 below, 37 below, 38–39, 40–41, 43 below, 48 above, 49 below, 70; Kenn Duncan 24 below; Fred Fehl 17 centre, 22–23 above, 23 below, 48 below, 66; John R Johnson 78–79; Hannes Kilian 76 above, 76 above, 76 below right; Serge Lido 20 above and below, 22–23 below, 24 above, 72 above and below, 73 above and below, 74 below; Novosti Press Agency 12, 33, 36, 69, 82–83 below; A Oxenham 80–81; David Palmer 80 above below left, 81; Fritz Peyer 74–75 above; Roger Pic 73 centre; The Scottish Ballet (Anthony Crickmay) endpapers, 62; Martha Swope Photography 1, 17 below, 19 right, 23 below, 29, 63, 64, 66–67, 67, 68 left and right; Syndication International 54, 58 below; Victoria and Albert Museum, Crown Copyright 8 left and right, 10, 11, 14 right, 15, 21, 45, 49 above; Wallace Collection, Crown Copyright 6–7; Woodmansterne Publications Ltd, Courtesy of The Royal Opera House, Covent Garden 28 right, 37 above.